GREAT GROUP GAMES

For Kids

150

Meaningful Activities for Any Setting

SUSAN RAGSDALE and **ANN SAYLOR**

SEARCH INSTITUTE PRESS

Great Group Games for Kids
150 Meaningful Activities for Any Setting

The following are registered trademarks of Search Institute: Search Institute®, Healthy Communities • Healthy Youth®, and Developmental Assets®.

Susan Ragsdale and Ann Saylor

Search Institute Press, Minneapolis, MN
Copyright © 2010 by Susan Ragsdale and Ann Saylor

The content of this book has been reviewed by a number of early childhood professionals. Every effort has been made to provide sound direction for each game described herein. The authors, publisher, and reviewers take no responsibility for the use or misuse of any materials or methods described in this book, and will not be held liable for any injuries caused by participating in activities and games from this book. Please use prudent judgment and take appropriate safety precautions when participating in all activities and games.

At the time of publication, all facts and figures cited herein are the most current available; all telephone numbers, addresses, and Web site URLs are accurate and active; all publications, organizations, Web sites, and other resources exist as described in this book; and all efforts have been made to verify them. The author and Search Institute make no warranty or guarantee concerning the information and materials given out by organizations or content found at Web sites that are cited herein, and we are not responsible for any changes that occur after this book's publication. If you find an error or believe that a resource listed herein is not as described, please contact Client Services at Search Institute.

10 9 8 7 6 5 4 3 2 1
Printed on acid-free paper in the United States of America.

Search Institute
615 First Avenue Northeast, Suite 125
Minneapolis, MN 55413
www.search-institute.org
612-376-9955 • 800-888-7828

ISBN-13: 978-1-57482-284-7

Credits
Book Design: Percolator
Production Supervisor: Mary Ellen Buscher

Library of Congress Cataloging-in-Publication Data
Ragsdale, Susan.
    Great group games for kids : 150 meaningful activities for any setting / Susan Ragsdale and Ann Saylor.
        p. cm.
    Includes index.
    ISBN-13: 978-1-57482-284-7 (pbk. : alk. paper)
    ISBN-10: 1-57482-284-5 (pbk. : alk. paper)
    1. Games. I. Saylor, Ann. II. Title.
GV1203.R336 2010
790.192′2--dc22
                                                2010013541

About Search Institute Press
Search Institute Press is a division of Search Institute, a nonprofit organization that offers leadership, knowledge, and resources to promote positive youth development. Our mission at Search Institute Press is to provide practical and hope-filled resources to help create a world in which all young people thrive. Our products are embedded in research, and the 40 Developmental Assets—qualities, experiences, and relationships youth need to succeed—are a central focus of our resources. Our logo, the SIP flower, is a symbol of the thriving and healthy growth young people experience when they have an abundance of assets in their lives.

To my three children, who inspire me to play every day—
in the classroom, on the playground, on the ball field, at
church, and in the backyard. Daniel, Brendan, and Anna
Kate, I love each of you tons and tons. To my dearest husband
and best friend, thank you for encouraging me to pursue my
dreams and supporting me every step of the way. —Ann

To Annie, Rob, Carol Anne ("Mom"), and Ray—
a promise kept and much thanks for all you've taught
and shared with me over the years. —Susan

Contents

Acknowledgments

In particular, we want to acknowledge and thank the following people for letting us uniquely fashion some of their games to fit this book:

"Balloon Ups and Downs" was adapted from a game shared by Amy Gallimore.

"Celebrity Dress-up" was created by 13-year-old Savannah Bobo-Bressler and her friends Kristina and Amanda McGinnis (and adapted by Aunt Susan with permission).

"Mr. Spider" was inspired by Joy Chapman.

"The Animal Game" and "The Entertainment Committee" were shared by Ashley Haupt, age 17.

"X-ray Vision" was inspired by Cindy Lawrence.

"Superhero Teams Relay Run" was created with Tracy Miller and Pete BoBo.

Tenessa, Bill, and Mary Ellen are the usual conspirators with whom we undertake the ongoing joy of producing a book at Search Institute Press. Karl, our new editor, it has been a treat. Without any of you, this book wouldn't exist. Truly. Literally. Each of you are "groovykins," and we are thankful that you like our ideas, tolerate our angst, are kind when you reject the ideas that just don't work, and make us look better than we really are. Thanks! And we have to appreciate our friends Cindy Lawrence and Bill Van De Griek for always being willing to test-drive some of our ideas to see how they fly. And to Melanie Jones, Kristin Murray, and Joy Chapman, who let us bounce ideas off them whenever we got stuck. Thanks, ladies! Thanks to Percolator for the cover and interior layout design.

Introduction

Play is the highest expression of human development in childhood, for it alone is the free expression of what is in a child's soul.
—**FRIEDRICH FROEBEL,** founder of modern kindergarten

Our previous games book, *Great Group Games: 175 Boredom-Busting, Zero-Prep Team Builders for All Ages*, was intended for a wide audience. Its games are playable within a variety of settings, and they are designed to be used by a broad range of age groups, from those in grade 3 to adults in a corporate setting. The book is a useful tool for clubs, conferences, offices, schools, retreats, college classes and campuses, places of worship, prisons, youth-serving agencies, and counseling centers across the country.

Once *Great Group Games* came out, we learned from those who used and loved the games. One thing we learned was that there were many teachers who were actively adapting the games for children younger than those in grade 3, and there was a desire for more activities specifically designed for youth in kindergarten through grade 5. From that feedback, we developed the idea for *Great Group Games for Kids*.

This book is crafted especially for those who work with children in K–5. That includes teachers, student teachers, child care workers, families throwing parties, youth workers in faith communities, after-school care providers, camp staff, sports and recreation leaders, youth leaders, and many others in related fields. If you work or interact with five or more children in this age range, you can find enjoyment and purpose in these pages, which will help you create environments where children are engaged, learning valuable skills and life lessons while having fun through *play development*. The games collected here were designed with child development principles in mind. For example, we have included games that teach children how to start conversations, build friendships, and play well together.

Finally, it should be noted that the games in this book can indeed be played by other age groups, but the reflection questions may need to be "bumped up" to reflect appropriate language and issues for them. No matter how young or old your participants may be, the games in this collection are easy to use and require little to no preparation.

Play and Learning

In trying to figure out how to introduce all the things we wanted to say about play that are so valuable to us, we decided to consult the poets. In perusing many great quotes about the value of play, games, and fun, we stumbled upon this poem by an unknown author:

> I tried to teach my child with books;
> He gave me only puzzled looks.
> I tried to teach my child with words;
> They passed him by often unheard.
> Despairingly, I turned aside;
> "How shall I teach this child?" I cried.
> Into my hand he put the key,
> "Come," he said, "play with me."

This poet had a child. He or she had experienced the pains of wanting to pass on something of value and worth to the precious little one and knew firsthand the frustration of wanting to impart wisdom and learning but running into dead ends. But the poet paid enough attention to the child to discover what many of us so often forget: that relationships and play hold the key.

This poem captures the spirit of play itself. Play is a means of discovery for children, and it gives prominence to life itself. To be sure, the love of play itself can and should be valued as its own gift. While playing, kids can totally immerse themselves in the game at hand and forget the world around them. When they are engaged in play, they experience the gift of presence and being free.

But play also results when wise teachers use their gift of engagement to encourage children to explore life questions, values, understanding, friendships, and self-awareness. Children have a natural curiosity that expresses itself through play. Play is one of the ways in which they learn about themselves, others, the world around them, and how it all works together.

"Come play with me," the child says. The child in the poem actually gives us two keys: play is the *way*; together is the *how*. The child could play alone, but he asks for the poet to play with him. Play is often more fun when others are involved. Play, then, also provides the necessary means for being together and building relationships.

This book carries those two principles at the heart of its understanding: play is the way in which children learn, and play provides the means through which we as adults can deepen our relationships with them.

But there is also a third principle woven into the pages of this book. We call it *play with purpose*, which is a personal mantra for our work. Play with purpose means tweaking a conversation about a game a little this way or a little that way to connect the game with a deeper purpose. As we have already said, there should be time and space for unstructured play, but there should also be time and space for play with purpose, where you direct the questions about the game ever so slightly to talk about life and its teachable moments.

Developmental Benefits

When we add the richness of Developmental Assets® to the tried-and-true formula of play, we have play with purpose. The Developmental Assets (which were created by Search Institute in Minneapolis, Minnesota) give us a picture of what a good, healthy life looks like for children. They spell out the relationships, influences, and factors that can have a positive impact on children's lives, helping those children develop their strengths and make healthy, responsible choices. When game leaders and developers deliberately think about and talk about these assets and include them in the mix, then purposeful play results. This kind of play honors the way children learn, builds thoughtful relationships, and is deliberately grounded in practices that focus on children's strengths and resources. (Visit www.search-institute.org/developmental-assets to see a complete list of the 40 Developmental Assets in English or Spanish.)

The Developmental Assets are divided into eight broad *asset categories*: Support, Empowerment, Boundaries and Expectations, Constructive Use of Time, Commitment to Learning, Positive Values, Social Competencies, and Positive Identity. Each game in this book is connected to these asset categories to help you better understand how you can create purposeful play. Review the list included here. Identifying the areas in which you want to do some more focused "play work" with your group can help you select the games that fit the particular needs of your players. The asset categories are organized as follows:

1. **Support**—Young people need to be surrounded by people who love, care for, appreciate, and accept them.

2. **Empowerment**—Young people need to feel valued and valuable. This happens when young people feel safe and respected.

3. **Boundaries and Expectations**—Young people need clear rules, consistent consequences for breaking rules, and encouragement to do their best.

4. **Constructive Use of Time**—Young people need opportunities—outside of school—to learn and develop new skills and interests with other youth and adults.

5. **Commitment to Learning**—Young people need a sense of the lasting importance of learning and a belief in their own abilities.

6. **Positive Values**—Young people need to develop strong guiding values or principles to help them make healthy life choices.

7. **Social Competencies**—Young people need the skills to interact effectively with others, to make difficult decisions, and to cope with new situations.

8. **Positive Identity**—Young people need to believe in their own self-worth and to feel that they have control over the things that happen to them.

When children are given an opportunity to develop these core values and skills through play, they will be better equipped to succeed in academics, leadership, and communication.

Adults engage children through play but youth can also be game leaders, and when it comes to play, that makes perfect sense. Young people are very effective in leading games and enjoy that responsibility. They often offer creative adaptations of old games with new relevance for today's issues. For example, Miranda Jones, age 13, shared how an old standby tag game that we knew as Blob Tag when we were growing up is still being played but is known in her youth group as the tag game H1N1. Same game, but with a new relevance, new understanding and context—defined by the youth themselves.

Those who encourage playtime for children know that it breaks down barriers and provides opportunities. They know from experience that play fosters relationship building—friendship building—and creates common ground among children from different neighborhoods, cultures, and age groups, who may have different interests, talents, and skill sets. Playtime provides a safe place for children to practice respect, responsibility, perseverance, and compassion, as well as develop and test new skills and competencies. It gives children a place to discover more about themselves and how they interact with others. In addition, it lets them experience life and teachable moments via mind, body, and spirit. It engages the whole of who they are.

When games hold children's interest—due no doubt to the fun factor and the relationships that the games help them build—and they keep coming back to your program, to your class, to your group, eager for more, *your* relationship with them has a chance to deepen and grow. As children continue to become more comfortable with you, two things happen: (1) you begin to influence how they spend their time, and (2) you continue to contribute to their sense of support as they realize that you are in their corner. Playing games is an excellent method for building assets and developing personal growth and positive relationships within your group.

As the game leader, you have the power of play in your hands. If you pay attention and make an effort to include the assets, then playtime can offer a pivotal experience of self-discovery and group growth, and you can contribute to the healthy developmental needs of children.

Playing with Purpose

This book is designed to help you play with purpose. The chapters are organized by key elements of child and group development that lend themselves to a natural progression in children's growth. We've organized the games as follows:

First Things First. Every group has a beginning, and the first step in any group is to learn other people's names and start using them. It is also necessary to create a space where children feel valued, safe, welcomed, and accepted. The games in this stage help establish connections, ensure that everyone is included, and provide opportunities for participants to get to know each other in fun ways.

Mixing Things Up. Once names are known and children begin to get comfortable, they are tempted to stick with the friends they've connected with and call it a day. Mixers keep things interesting and provide opportunities for children to work with lots of other people and expand their friendship base.

Friendship Starters. All friendships take work, but it's not necessarily intuitive for children (or even adults!) to know how to "grow" friendships. How do you move beyond simply knowing a name? How do you build friendships? This section offers games for children to learn and practice friendship skills through conversation starters and games that further develop their social skills.

Relationship Builders. Building relationships is an ongoing process. And within that process are key aspects that can enhance or diminish relationships, including the dynamics of a group, personality details, and the appreciation of diversity. This section offers a variety of games that develop an understanding and appreciation of these relationship boosters.

Team Play. Games in this section help children begin to learn *how* to work together as a group. A wide variety of games provide opportunities for children to continue to have fun and practice elementary cooperation and interactive skills.

Expressing Values through Play. Developing values takes time. Games can provide the venue for children to begin to question, prod, and understand what values are and what those values mean to them personally. They can begin to set and claim their own values with an understanding of why those values are important for them and how they can become the kind of people they want to be. These games create the kind of space and probing children need to examine values.

Elements of Challenge. These games encourage players to expand their own sense of being comfortable with themselves and to take risks. The problem-solving tasks put forth provide challenges both for individuals to face alone and for teams to work on together. In both cases, players must risk their own opinions and test their own worth as they resolve conflicts, cooperate, and face obstacles.

Celebrations. Each group offers up moments to celebrate, both collectively and as individuals within the group. It is important to watch for, identify, and lift up the celebratory moments that present themselves. Celebrating reinforces a positive sense of self and an appreciation for life's gifts. The games in this section offer simple ways to honor the group, individual, and team talents; emphasize group learning; and celebrate group identity.

Another way this book will help you play with purpose is through the Going Deeper reflection questions, which are listed at the end of most of the games. Feel free to select the Going Deeper questions that work best with your group and the amount of time you have, or use them as inspiration for your own discussion points. They are designed to help you lead a conversation with the group that helps participants apply their game-time experience to real life—their own lives, to be exact. When you are debriefing using the Going Deeper questions, talk about the game first: "What did you think?" "What did you like?" "What did you not like?" "How was it fun?" "In what way was it challenging?" Then talk about what participants experienced in the game. Finally, connect the game to the real world, real life: "How does this apply to our lives?" "What can we learn from this game and use elsewhere?"

Additionally, each game is linked to several asset categories to help you see the child development aspect you are helping forge when you play that particular game. You can place additional emphasis on these aspects with more discussion if you so choose.

Game Tips

DIVIDING TEAMS WITH AN UNEVEN NUMBER OF PLAYERS
If you have an uneven number of players when you are trying to split into teams, you might consider one of these solutions:

- Let one pair become a triad.
- Ask an adult helper to "sit out" for the activity.
- Ask an adult helper to "step in" to make the groups even.
- Ask one child to be your assistant (or the leader) for the activity.
- If it's a team activity, let one player on the smaller team participate twice.

ARE *YOU* READY TO PLAY? A GAME LEADER'S CHECKLIST
The description for each game details everything you need to play the game—time, supplies, preparation, instructions, and debriefing questions (Going Deeper).

- Before game time, look over the instructions for the game(s) you're going to play. Make sure you're familiar with the instructions and have a good sense of how things work. If you're prepared, the game will go a lot more smoothly.

- Does the game require supplies? Look under *Supplies* within each game description. Many of the games in this book require no props, but if they are needed, they will be listed there. Gather any needed supplies and set them aside in a place where you'll be able to find them easily.

- Does the game require any preparatory work? Those that do will be highlighted in the game description under *Prep*.

- Is the area ready for play? Make sure everything is safe, set up the perimeter of the play area, and have your materials available and organized.

- Does the game require extra assistance? Gather any extra people you might need to help as coaches, judges, supporters, or demonstrators. Tell them about their roles before game time so that you'll be ready to play when the children arrive.

KNOW YOUR PLAY SPACE

Most of the games in this book can be played indoors or outdoors, but knowing the limitations and benefits of the space where you will be playing games is a "must" in order to think through safety factors and any factors that might get in the way of the game accomplishing its mission. This is especially important if you are taking your group to a place other than where you normally meet. Consider the following:

- Is the area large enough for the group to play the game you've selected?

- Is the area safe for players? Are tree roots or holes in the way? Are structural columns or furniture blocking the space? Are there exposed nails or other hazards to be avoided? Is the ceiling falling apart? (Yes, it does happen!)

- Will all players be easily visible during the game at all times? If not, do they need to be?

- Will your group's noise disturb others?

- Is the space quiet enough for participants to focus?

- Do you have access to restrooms and drinking fountains?

● If you are outside, are you prepared for the weather? Is there a back-up space just in case rain or snow forces you inside?

KNOW WHO'S PLAYING

As you choose your games, consider the physical, emotional, intellectual, and social abilities of your players, or be prepared to make adaptations to help the game meet your group's goals. For example, if someone has vision problems, you might need an extra guide to work with that individual on a task. If someone is in a wheelchair, you might need to allow extra space for maneuvering, or let the walking members of your group crabwalk or walk backward to slow them down a bit. Just remember to set the stage in such a way that the adaptation becomes part of the challenge or setting. You don't want to embarrass anyone.

If you choose a game that entails sensitive conversations, set your expectations for respect upfront, and invite other caring adults to help monitor the game. If your group can't yet read or write at the level of the game, consider ways to play the game verbally instead of using paper. You know your group best, so take time to think about any special considerations for their playtime, and make the necessary preparations.

Remember, the goal is to actively engage players in games that build on their strengths and help them to work together. Special considerations can often lend opportunities to meet those goals head-on.

KEEPING CONTROL

One of the tricks of the trade in leading games is figuring out how *you* are going to control the group once you've turned participants loose to talk to each other and share. Not all of us are naturally blessed with a booming, commanding voice that elicits instant silence or rapt attention.

Here are some of the methods we've used, learned, or seen in action that can help gather the players' attention when you're ready for them to complete the task at hand and turn their attention back to you for the next great thing.

First and foremost, establish a signal that will let the group know it's time for "attention up front" with quiet voices. The key is to practice it with your group, to make sure they understand. Ensuring that they all know your signal will help you get their immediate attention when you need it—whether you are cuing the next activity or addressing a safety issue.

There are various methods you can use to establish your signal. You might use the traditional "shh" finger to your lips or raise a hand in the sky. Sometimes that's all it takes. Sometimes you might need a different method.

Another method is to tell participants the time limit they'll have to talk or do the task at hand. Give time checks along the way: "You have five more minutes." "Three more minutes." "One more minute." "30 seconds." At 10 seconds, start the countdown, out loud: "Ten, nine, eight, seven, six, five, four, three, two, one. Okay, let's focus attention up here." Often, simply counting out loud is enough because participants start tuning in to you.

For the times when a countdown doesn't work (or if you have a soft voice that doesn't carry), try these additional enhancements to let everyone know when time is up:

- Flick the lights several times or dim them until voices soften.

- Use a train whistle (preferable to a coach's whistle because its notes are softer and not so jarring).

- *But* if the group is outside, the coach's whistle might be better. It also may be useful when the group is too rambunctious and rowdy.

- Create your own verbal interruption: "If you hear my voice, clap once; if you hear my voice, clap twice; if you hear my voice, clap three times." The participants who hear you will respond. As *they* respond with claps, others start to tune in. If you don't have everyone by three claps, you'll need to reinforce with the group that listening is a key part of playing. Find what works.

- Live music: Get a few participants near you to join you in humming some tune, such as the *Addams Family* theme song (which involves snapping one's fingers) to get attention.

- Taped music: Tell participants on the front end that when they hear the music come on, they should stop what they're doing. Pick a song that is definitely not background music but something that will get their attention, and turn it on. Or go the other way, and find a song that matches the amount of time you want them to play, turn it on, and when the song finishes, so should they.

- Mimic the school bell: This is a familiar sound and reference point for starting and stopping an activity. "Ding, ding, ding! Ding, ding, ding! Time is up!"

- Clocks: Set the timer or timers, and have clocks go off when the time is up.

When we were working on this book, our friend Cindy told us about her recent experiment in getting the attention of a grade 4 class. She was the special guest in the classroom. She simply walked up to the front of the room, without being introduced, and stood before them, tapping the top of her head while bobbing it back and forth. A few children joined her in doing the action. She changed the physical action to something else. More joined her. She kept mixing up what she was doing until every single child quieted down and started mimicking what she was doing. She had them. They then started the lesson.

It just goes to show: there are many ways to get attention. It all has to do with our personalities, presence, and creativity! Use what works!

CIRCLE UP!

Why do game leaders often have groups circle up? Gathering your group into a circle puts into play several things all at the same time:

- First, it taps into something familiar. As young children, we are often accustomed to playing games that start in a circle, such as Duck, Duck, Goose or Ring around the Rosie. The hope is that a circle is a familiar position that brings with it good memories and signifies that it's time to play.

- Second, being in a circle removes any physical barriers. There is nothing to distance you, as the game leader, from the players, and there is nothing to distance them from each other—no desks, no books, no chairs. You are all together.

- Third, it pushes against any internal barriers. Standing shoulder to shoulder, or even in close proximity, starts to melt the barriers that people build between themselves and others. You and the players next to you are rubbing elbows, and soon you'll be doing something together that relies on all of you as a team.

- Circling up also gives you a freebie in the way of assistance—you get the distinct advantage of being able to look at every participant eye to eye. There's no hiding in the circle, not behind books, or desks, or other people. Everyone shows up—ready or not.

Add all that together, and you have a circle with no distinct beginning or ending, where everyone is in the same space. Distractions have been removed. Distinctions are minimized—the circle is made of the people in it and what they bring to the game. Whatever happens next will be created by all of you—together.

KNOW HOW TO ADDRESS SERIOUS CONCERNS APPROPRIATELY

It's amazing how games break down barriers and encourage children to share their feelings. And that's a great thing! We want to help children know their own feelings and learn how to deal with them—good and bad. Part of the play development process is to help build social and emotional competencies. However, if children ever share information that causes you to wonder about their emotional or physical safety, find a time to ask them about it quietly, one on one. Support them through their challenges. If something really unexpected and unfortunate comes up that requires further investigation, follow your agency's protocols for keeping children safe.

WHEN ARE YOU PLAYING?

Games in this book range from calm and quiet to loud and active. As you choose the game that best fits your day, think through your agenda and what you'll be doing. Do you need to:

- Boost energy in the middle of your agenda? In the middle of a class or meeting?
- Focus your group's attention on the task at hand?
- Fill the whole day with activities?
- Have a time of laughter and celebration?
- Encourage one another and strengthen the spirit of the team?
- Take a break and mix things up?

Knowing when and where to use games, as well as why, will help you pick the right games to enhance your time with your players.

COMPETITION IS OPTIONAL

Games don't always have to be about winning! If your group gets too aggressive with competition, or the competition aspect detracts attention from the learning aspect, then don't compete!

Instead, make it about *personal bests*. For example, a relay doesn't have to be about which team finishes first—it can be about how each team improves its overall time with each stage of the game. At which stage did the team excel? Where did its members find their strengths as a team? Where did they improve as they focused and applied effort?

Individual events don't have to be about competition either. They, too, can be about personal bests. For example, Paper-Wad Fun (see pages 121–122) doesn't have to applaud the player who scores the most points. Instead, you can twist it around to encourage participants to keep track of individual progress and aim for their own personal bests.

Game Shortcuts

SHORTCUT #1

For games that require starting and/or finish lines or boundaries, consider these options to see what you have on hand that might save money and effort:

- **Chalk:** You can use chalk to mark the lines.

- **Tape:** Traditionally, masking tape is used to mark lines, but electrical tape also works well for outside games.

- **Ropes:** Lay rope down on the floor for players to line up behind.

- **Traffic cones:** Set orange cones in a line, and have each team line up beside one.

- **Chairs:** Set chairs in place to mark boundaries or to create the point from which players start or finish.

- **Paper plates, wood scraps, bases,** or **cardboard pieces:** Place these simple objects in corners to mark boundaries or on the edges of starting/finish lines for participants to visually note and run past.

- **People:** Children who are sick, injured, or in "time-out" can be the human boundaries or line markers, holding out their hands for players to tag before they start or when they are finishing.

SHORTCUT #2

Sometimes a game calls for a variety of colored candies, usually for the sake of dividing groups by colors or to match colors with a question or activity. Here are a variety of other options to consider that might save calories or that might simply involve items that are on sale or on hand:

- **Froot Loops, M&M's, SweeTarts:** Groups can be divided according to a child's maximum number of any individual color, or questions can be matched to the various colors.

- **Chex Mix or trail mix:** Match the item to the question ("If you have a pretzel, answer this . . .") *or* match the maximum amount of a certain item ("I have 10 peanuts") to the group players should form ("Who else has more peanuts than any other item?").

- **Shapes:** Use various LEGO bricks, building blocks, shapes (triangles, squares, rectangles, etc.) to divide the group into like shapes or to control the questions being asked.

- **Lollipops/suckers/hard candy:** Divide by color or type.

- **Scraps of cloth, colored paper:** Pull these from a hat and divide groups by the color of the items, or have players answer a particular question based on the color or type of scrap paper they have.
- **Colored stickers:** Put stickers on children's name tags, hands, or shirts.

SHORTCUT #3

How can you take one game and keep its core goal but give it a different look? How can you make it just a tad bit different each time and create five games out of one? A games master can play the same game with participants three to five times, and they won't get bored. "Creative adaptability" is called for when you realize you don't *have* the supplies on hand and you have to think quickly about how to make the game work, because it's almost time to play and the group is getting restless.

Look at "Build a Tower" (pages 184–185). The goal is to build the highest freestanding tower possible using newspaper and masking tape. Here are some potential ways to adapt this game by using different supplies to build the tower:

- Straws and paper clips—this version allows you to use tabletops if space is an issue
- Marshmallows and toothpicks—this, too, lets you take advantage of smaller spaces
- Construction paper and regular tape
- Pretzels and marshmallows

Empowerment—and Fun!

Remember, playing games always provides opportunities to make "play with purpose" connections. Every time an icebreaker is played, players get to know each other better, and they build a sense of support and safety. When clear expectations and boundaries are adhered to in games, players learn the value behind having rules and the reasons why they're so important. When games offer challenge, children grow. As they stretch themselves and take risks, they begin to feel empowered to try to accomplish more. And of course, the whole group can have a lot of fun in the process.

Ready, set, play!

First Things First:
Who *Are* These People?

The true object of all human life is play.
—**G. K. CHESTERTON,** English writer

In the development of any group of people, whether they are adults, teenagers, or children, there is a first step. In our first book, *Great Group Games*, we dubbed that first stage "starting off right." When you boil that idea down to its most basic of steps, you get to first things first: Who's in the room? Who *are* these people? And "they"—the other participants in the room—are wondering the exact same thing: "Who's *that*?" They may be feeling a combination of excitement and curiosity mingled with fear and uncertainty.

When you are taking care of business, the first step in sorting the various bodies before you into individuals with faces and personalities that you begin to recognize and remember is all about *names*. (Of course this also helps them get to know each other and begin to like each other.)

The first thing to practice when you are crafting a space where children feel valued, safe, welcomed, and accepted is learning their names and using them. Being named and being known are powerful—so much so that it is worth repeating: *being named and being known are powerful.*

Being named is the first step in recognizing our identity—we exist, we are, we are here, we are important to somebody, we matter. Calling someone by name, using that person's name, says, "I see you. I recognize you. I know you are here." It's the first step in giving value to the people with whom we interact.

The name games in this chapter help you do just that: recognize and know each other while getting comfortable and feeling at ease all at the same time. Ranging from quiet, individual conversations to action-packed, fast-paced movement, the various approaches of the different games in this chapter give you numerous options that each help you take care of first things first. Play more than one name game in a single gathering to ensure maximum mingling time. Or, if time is a factor, play often over the course of several gatherings until you can see that participants aren't struggling to call each other by name.

Birthday Scramble

TIME
5–10 minutes

SUPPLIES

- Enough chairs for every player except one person

THE GAME Have the group sit in a circle of chairs. Have one player be "it" and stand in the middle of the circle (that person doesn't have a seat in the circle). The person who is "it" can call out any two months of the year or any two numbers between 1 and 31—or a combination thereof. If any seated players have a birthday either on that date or in that month, they should get up, yell out their names, and scramble for a new seat. At the same time, "it" should also try to take over one of the vacated seats. The person left in the middle is the new "it." The big move is when "it" chooses to yell out "Happy birthday, everyone!" At that point, everyone should scramble for a new seat.

GOING DEEPER

- In this game, we threw our names out there, but it was difficult to really keep track of all the names. Is it easy or hard to learn other people's names?

- What about meeting others? Is that hard or easy?

- Who feels really comfortable introducing her- or himself to others? (Ask for a show of hands, and then ask if anyone would share tips for making introductions easier.)

Review the aspects of polite introductions: shake hands, make eye contact, speak clearly, and ask for the other person's name as well.

ASSET CATEGORIES: Support, Social Competencies, Positive Identity

Name Song

TIME
5 minutes

SUPPLIES

- Chalkboard and chalk or a flip chart and markers

PREP On the board or flip chart, make a list of emotions that describe how players might feel today. Words should be one syllable so that they fit into the last line of the children's song "Frère Jacques." You might include words such as *fine, great, glad, blue, sad, mad, sick,* and so on.

THE GAME Teach players the lead and response melodies for the following lyrics using the tune to the children's song "Frère Jacques." Once they have the song down, go around the group and have each player say her or his name.

Players: Who is _____? Who is _____? *[Fill in one of the names of the players in the group.]*

Identified player sings back and waves a hand at everyone: That is me! That is me!

Players: How are you to-day? How are you to-day?

Identified player: I feel _____ *[Let them fill in a word from the list on the board.]* I feel _____.

NOTE The song "Frère Jacques" is originally sung in French; the English version is generally known as "Are You Sleeping?"

GOING DEEPER

- Why is it important for us to take the time to learn names?
- Why is it important for us to be able to express how we're feeling?
- How can we help others when they're not having a good day? How can we be a good influence on them?
- What if *we're* the ones not having a good day? What can we do to turn things around?

- A person's attitude can have a huge effect on the spirit of a group. Give a thumbs-up if you think the following attitudes are good for our group and a thumbs-down if you think they might hurt our group: Happy? Grumpy? Selfish? "Making the best" of a situation? Mean? Complaining? Helpful? Funny?

Tactfully follow up on any feelings that need exploring—if someone felt sad or mad. This can be done individually or within the group. ("Why do you feel sad?" "What can we do to help make this a good day?")

ASSET CATEGORIES: Support, Constructive Use of Time, Social Competencies, Positive Identity

Name That Person!

TIME
5–10 minutes

THE GAME Have the group sit in a circle. Go around the circle and have everyone say her or his own name out loud. Designate one player to be "it." That individual should stand in the middle of the circle. He or she will look around the circle, arbitrarily point at another player, and say, "Name that person on your left" or "Name that person on your right." The player who is "it" will then count to five out loud and as fast as possible. The player who was pointed at should name the person on his or her left (or right, if that was the direction called) *before* "it" reaches the end of a five count. If that player can't, then he or she trades places with the person in the middle and becomes the new "it." Have players change positions in the circle from time to time to keep things interesting.

GOING DEEPER
- Does knowing names make you feel more comfortable in a group?
- This game put you on the spot. You had to name names fast! How do you handle pressure (being on the spot) when it comes to taking tests? How do you feel when your friends want to do something you don't want to do?

- What helps you to remain cool when you are in a tough spot?
- How can you help your friends when they are under pressure?

Cartoon Names

TIME
10–15 minutes

THE GAME Ask players to gather into one big circle (unless the group has more than 15 people, in which case you could organize them into smaller groups of 6–10). Have players go around the circle one at a time and introduce themselves, sharing their first names *and* their favorite cartoon characters. For example, the first player, George, might say, "George Superman." Everyone else in the circle should repeat "George Superman" and then go to the next person and repeat the process. Eventually the group will go around the circle saying each person's cartoon name.

A variation for this game would be to have the players swap positions in the circle and then see if anyone can still remember everyone's cartoon name. Let one or two people try to remember. Then the participants as a group should try to say everyone's cartoon name.

GOING DEEPER

- Why did you pick the cartoon character that you did? What are some of the things you like about that character?
- What is one thing you hope others will like or remember about you?
- Did this game help you learn and remember names? What helps you remember new things?
- Did you discover others in the group who like the same things you do? Would sharing something in common help people feel more comfortable with each other?

Super Names

TIME
10–15 minutes

THE GAME Have players gather into one big circle (unless the group has more than 15 participants, in which case you could break them into smaller groups of 6–10). Tell them that you have just discovered you have a room full of superheroes in the making. You want to know what makes each of them super. Are they super nice? Super fast? Super strong? Have players go around the circle and introduce themselves one at a time by stating their first names *and* how they are super. The first player might say, "I'm Chloe, and I try to be super helpful." Continue around the circle. At the end, players should say everyone's names and what makes them super.

For older children, ask them to add a motion to their superpower. For example, if Antonio says he's super fast, he might choose to run in place. Then ask the whole group to repeat Antonio's name and run in place as they note his superpower. ("This is Antonio, and he's super fast.") Repeat with each person.

NOTE A child might have trouble thinking of a way he or she is super. For instance, if Johnny isn't sure how to respond, you might ask the other children how they see Johnny trying to be super, or you might share one way that you see Johnny trying to be super.

GOING DEEPER

- Why did you pick the characteristic that you did?
- In what ways can you be super each day? How can you show super behavior, express super attitudes, or be a super example?
- What is one thing you hope others will like about you (or remember about you)?
- Did this game help you learn and remember names? What helps you remember new things?

ASSET CATEGORIES: Commitment to Learning, Social Competencies, Positive Identity

Mission: Names Icebreaker

TIME
5–10 minutes

SUPPLIES

- Paper, a pen, and a standard envelope
- Music on CD or MP3 (such as the *Inspector Gadget* or *Mission: Impossible* theme songs)
- CD player or MP3 player with speakers
- Manila envelope
- A watch with a timer

PREP Write down the following message and place it in the standard envelope:

I need your help! In this room are some very special people. You must find them. They have to be identified. Go to someone you don't know. Introduce yourself and share something special about yourself. Then find out the other person's name and something special about her or him. After you've exchanged information, hand her or him the package. That person must then introduce her- or himself to someone else and hand the package off. Continue on. Hurry! This package will self-destruct in four minutes.

THE GAME Start the music to set a fun atmosphere for the game, and designate a couple of people to gather the group together. Once they are assembled, tell them that you have just received a package and an envelope addressed to the group in the room. Ask someone to open the standard envelope and read its message to the others out loud. While the others are listening to the message, discreetly set the timer on the watch to four minutes, start it running, put it into the manila envelope, and fasten the envelope. This is the "package." When the person reading the message has finished delivering the instructions to the rest of the group, hand the package to him or her.

The group should immediately begin introductions. When the timer goes off, whoever is caught with the package in her or his hands should be led to the center of the room and placed in a seat of honor. If the group desires to have introductions continue, reset the watch alarm and continue mingling. Each player caught by the self-destruct timer should join the middle.

After several rounds are finished, the remaining players should gather around the honored guests, who will then introduce themselves to the rest of the group and share something special about themselves with everyone.

GOING DEEPER

- How did it feel to share with others what you think makes you special? How did it feel to talk about yourself?
- What was something neat you learned about someone else?
- In this game, all participants share something special about themselves. What is something that makes this group special as a whole?
- How did it feel to be in the spotlight?

ASSET CATEGORIES: Support, Social Competencies, Positive Identity

Who's Coming to Snacks and Play?

TIME
10–15 minutes

THE GAME Have the group form a circle. Tell the children that you are inviting them over to eat snacks and play, and you want to know who is coming and what they are bringing. They should introduce themselves and name either a snack they're bringing *or* a game they will lead at playtime. Whether they name a snack or a game, it should begin with the same letter as their first name. For example, Ben might want to lead basketball, so he's Basketball Ben. Once he introduces himself, everyone should repeat "Basketball Ben." Next in line might be Cathy, and she's bringing crackers for snacks, so everyone will start at the beginning and say, "Basketball Ben" and then "Crackers Cathy." Continue around the circle until everyone has been introduced.

GOING DEEPER

- How confident do you feel that you now know everyone's name? (If someone is confident, you can offer the opportunity for that person to try to name everyone.)

- Is it easier to approach others and make friends once you know names? Why or why not?

- What are other ways that you like to play when you have the chance?

ASSET CATEGORIES: Support, Constructive Use of Time, Social Competencies

Drum Beat Name Game

TIME
10–15 minutes

THE GAME Sit in a circle. Establish a solid four-beat rhythm using these hand motions: *pat, pat, snap, snap*. (For the "pat, pat" motion children pat their legs with their hands, and for "snap, snap" they snap their fingers.) On the first snap beat, the lead player should say his name, followed by another player's name said on the second snap beat. The player whose name is called with the second snap beat will repeat her name on the next snap, along with a third player's name on the second snap. For example, Joe would pat, pat, and then say his name during the first snap and another player's name, Nancy, during the second snap (*pat, pat*, "Joe, Nancy"). Then Nancy would say her name during the next snap, followed by Trinity's name during her second snap (*pat, pat*, "Nancy, Trinity").

If a player misses a beat or says the wrong name, that person gets a strike against him or her. After two strikes, a player becomes a judge on the outside of the circle. Those players still in the circle will restart play, omitting the names of those who have been called out. The judges observe the remaining players, and they can make a funny "buzzer" sound when one of the players makes a mistake. The last remaining player wins the game.

NOTE If players don't know how to snap yet, they can just move their fingers in a snapping motion.

GOING DEEPER

- How did it feel to be called by name in this activity?
- How does it make you feel when a new person remembers your name?
- This game requires lots of concentration. In what other activities do you need this skill?
- This game also requires quick thinking. Is that easy or hard for you? When is it important to think and speak very quickly?

ASSET CATEGORIES: Support, Commitment to Learning, Social Competencies

Rhyming Names

TIME
15 minutes

THE GAME Gather the group in a circle. Ask players to introduce themselves to the group, one by one, by stating their name and sharing a word that rhymes with their name. For example, players might say, "Ann's van," "Kate's late," "Daniel's spaniel," "Susan's cruisin'," and so on. The group responds to each person's introduction by repeating the name and rhyming word to affirm the person and learn the name. As each new person introduces her- or himself, ask the group to also repeat each previous person's name and rhyming word. Eventually the whole group will be repeating every player's name and rhyming word.

NOTE Some names may be difficult to rhyme. In such situations, it would be acceptable for players to create their own nonsense words that *do* rhyme with those names. Other players could help think of rhymes as well, as long as they provide respectful suggestions.

GOING DEEPER

- What were the funniest or craziest rhymes you heard in the game?

- What was the hardest part of this game?

- This is a great way to remember names. How do you remember other things? For instance, how do you remember to pack your goggles after swimming, or take your raincoat home when the rain has passed, or put away all your toys when you're finished playing?

- Why is it important to remember the names of the people in our group?

ASSET CATEGORIES: Support, Empowerment, Commitment to Learning, Social Competencies

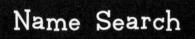

TIME

10 minutes

SUPPLIES

- A preformatted word-search grid that includes the first names of all players (one per player)

PREP Prepare the word-search grid with all the players' names. Do not provide a list of the names included in the grid unless this is the group's first time to meet each other. The following is an example of a word-search grid featuring the names Mary, Mandy, Matt, Nate, and Yvone:

M	A	R	Y	L
A	A	B	R	S
N	A	T	E	G
D	I	W	T	F
Y	V	O	N	E

(Tip: There are several Web sites that provide free online tools to help users create word-search puzzles.)

THE GAME Distribute a word-search handout to each player. Challenge players to find and circle the first names of each player inside the grid. When a person finishes, he or she should say, "Search complete." After the first five to seven players finish, tell everyone that it is now a group word search. Let all the players, in turn, stand, share their names, and point out where their names are located on the grid. Players can circle their names as they share them.

NOTE If a player is unable to find her or his own name by the time the others are ready to share, you could give that person time to search while others are sharing, or you could allow others to help her or him.

GOING DEEPER

- What were the secrets to success in this game?
- Some people think it's easier to list all the players' names, then search for them in the grid. When you are given a complex task, what do you do to make it easier?
- What's one new name you've learned that you'll be certain to remember?

- Sometimes searching for things is very difficult. Whether you're searching for a lost shoe or your missing cat or the answer to a math problem, hunting takes a lot of determination. What do I mean by "determination"?

- How will a sense of determination help you succeed in school? In sports? In life?

ASSET CATEGORIES: Support, Commitment to Learning, Positive Values, Social Competencies

Fill It Up

TIME
5–10 minutes

SUPPLIES

- Preprinted list of actions ("Fill It Up" card) for people to collect from others (one list and one pencil per person)

PREP Create a Fill It Up card by typing out a list of actions with spaces for players to add their initials, or visit ➊ www.search-institute.org/great-group-games-for-kids to download a printable Fill It Up card.

THE GAME Distribute a Fill It Up card to each player. Challenge all players to mingle and complete all the things listed on their card as fast as possible. The player who completes the card the fastest is the winner. Verify all the facts on the winner's card by having that person introduce the other players and identify which spaces they match on the card.

NOTE Each person should sign each card only one time, unless you have fewer players than places for initials. In that situation, you might allow one or two people to sign a card twice. An alternative to sample challenge number five on the Fill It Up card, particularly for non-coed groups, would be for each player to shake another player's hand.

GOING DEEPER

- How did you help each other in this game?
- Why is it important to take the time to learn names, even when you are doing tasks?
- What did you learn about your teammates during this game?
- You made a silly memory with many of the other players. After making memories with others, are you more or less likely to treat them

kindly? To help them when they are in need? To share with them? To stick up for them?

- In the game, you had power to help other players succeed by giving your time and silliness. In real life, how can you help others succeed?

ASSET CATEGORIES: Support, Empowerment, Constructive Use of Time, Positive Values, Social Competencies

Hot Potato Jumble

TIME
5–10 minutes

SUPPLIES

- A tossable object (such as a beanbag) and music or a timer

THE GAME Gather all players into a circle. The group is going to pass around the tossable object, which is considered the hot potato. The players will say their names when they get it, and then they will pass it on to the nearest person. If you are using a timer, set it for 10–20 seconds. You can also use recorded music and plan to stop it after 10–20 seconds of play. When you turn off the music or the timer sounds, whoever is holding the hot potato has to answer one question about her- or himself, such as "What is your favorite color?" or "What animal would you most like to have as a pet?" That person then steps out of the circle for the remainder of the game, but she or he can still watch and think of questions to ask. Questions can come from anyone in the group, whether they are inside or outside of the circle.

Play resumes with the player who would have been next to receive the hot potato if the music hadn't stopped, and the game continues, allowing everyone the chance to be in the "hot spot" and answer a question, until only one player is left.

GOING DEEPER

- How did it feel to be caught with the hot potato and to have to answer an unknown question?
- What surprising or interesting thing did you learn about someone else?
- What did you learn about asking questions to find out more about others?
- How are questions important in developing friendships and finding common interests?
- What are some questions that you could ask others, if you wanted to get to know them a little bit better?

ASSET CATEGORIES: Support, Commitment to Learning, Social Competencies, Positive Identity

TIME
5 minutes

SUPPLIES

- Paper and a pen for each person

THE GAME Players should write down responses to the following prompts:

1. Something about their appearance today (for example, *wearing red* or *have on jeans*).

2. Something about their character (*I like to laugh, I am nice, I am honest, I make others laugh,* etc.).

3. Something unique about them or that they have done (*I've gone fishing, I earned an A in math, I can chew gum and blow a bubble within a bubble*).

4. Their name.

Collect all the papers from everyone, choose one, and slowly read out information about the person one item at a time. When the first three facts have been read, ask the other players for guesses as to which person is being described. After a few guesses, ask the person of the moment to stand, and introduce her or him to the rest of the group.

You can choose to read all the papers one day, or as desired over time.

GOING DEEPER

- What did you enjoy learning about others?
- How important is it to develop your own character?
- Why is it important to be able to appreciate what makes you unique?
- How important is it to feel good about yourself and have good self-esteem?
- How can you celebrate what makes you special or the special things you have done in life that were fun and meaningful?
- How can you help others feel good about themselves?

ASSET CATEGORIES: Support, Positive Values, Social Competencies, Positive Identity

TIME
15–20 minutes

SUPPLIES

- One die (big fuzzy dice are especially fun)

THE GAME Have volunteers come up one at a time and roll the die. See what number comes out on top. The players who roll the die should give their name and tell several facts about themselves (or things they like to do) in relation to the number they roll. For example, if they roll a six, they should tell six things about themselves. If players have trouble coming up with things to say about themselves, the other players can prompt them with questions.

GOING DEEPER

- Did you discover that you have things in common with someone else?

- What other questions could we ask each other to get to know each other better?

- How did listening play a big role in this game?

- Why is it important to take time to get to know others and build friendships?

- Were you nervous about talking out loud in the group? What might give you courage to speak up in the future?

ASSET CATEGORIES: Support, Empowerment, Social Competencies, Positive Identity

Colorful Characters

TIME
5–10 minutes

THE GAME For this game, you could split the group into pairs or small groups, although you could also stay together as a big group. Have all players introduce themselves in turn and finish the statement: "If I were a color, I would be the color _____, because _____."

NOTE If you want to add another element to the game, challenge participants to group themselves into four corners based on similar colors, then ask the corner groups to write a poem about their color.

GOING DEEPER

- Are there any persons in the room for whom you would have picked a different color than they did? Who are they and what colors would you have picked for them? Why would you have picked those colors? For instance, you might say, "Justin has tons of energy, so I think of him as orange," or "Sally is always cheery, so I think of her as sunshiny yellow."

- What do you think the colors people picked say about who they are? Do the colors match their personalities?
- Sometimes people say that they "see red" or "feel blue." How can colors let you express important feelings?

ASSET CATEGORIES: Support, Empowerment, Social Competencies

Musical Matches

TIME
5–10 minutes

SUPPLIES
- Two lines of chairs facing each other some distance apart to allow for movement (one chair per person)
- Music and music player (a portable stereo, for example)

THE GAME Divide the group into two teams. Assign each team one of the lines of chairs. When you're ready, ask the group a question of your choice, but tell them not to answer just yet. Instead, start the music and instruct participants to walk in a circular path around their line of chairs. When the music stops, they should each scramble for a seat. Now, players should be seated and facing someone from the other team. Each pair should introduce themselves and answer the question you posed to the group. Rotate as often as desired by playing music and mixing up the directions. You could let each line rotate or shuffle people around into different lines just to shake things up.

To add an element of challenge, have whoever sits down last be the one who thinks up a question for discussion.

Possible questions:

- What is one thing you enjoy learning about at school?
- What is one thing you like to do in your spare time?
- What is your favorite kind of cookie?

- Who is the ultimate superhero?
- Which TV star would you most like to meet and why?
- What is one of your favorite music groups or songs?
- If you had to perform before a group of people, what would you do? Would you sing, act, tell jokes, or read something you wrote yourself?
- What is something good that has happened to you this week?

GOING DEEPER

- Did you discover you and other players had things in common that you didn't know about beforehand?
- How do you feel differently about someone after they know something about you besides your name?
- How does talking about fun things help in building friendships?
- What is one thing you learned from playing this game?
- After hearing other people's answers to the questions, what is something new that you would like to experience?

ASSET CATEGORIES: Support, Commitment to Learning, Social Competencies, Positive Identity

Nicknames Chronicles

TIME
10 minutes

THE GAME Divide the group into teams of two or three people. Invite players to share one of their nicknames with their small groups, and share a story behind their nickname. If some players don't have nicknames, or if they don't want to share their nicknames, invite them to create their own positive nicknames for themselves. If people want to, invite them to share their nicknames with the large group.

GOING DEEPER

- What are some favorite nicknames that you heard today?
- Why do we give nicknames to one another?
- Is it ever wrong to use someone's nickname?
- How can you be sensitive about the names you call one another?

ASSET CATEGORIES: Support, Positive Values, Social Competencies, Positive Identity

Mixing Things Up

Deep meaning lies often in childish play.
—JOHANN FRIEDRICH VON SCHILLER, German poet and philosopher

Once players start making connections, they have a tendency to stay with the people they first meet or the people they really like. It's human nature. If you find a safe place and latch on, or find someone you like, then why move on? You've made a friend. It's time to hang out and enjoy.

We want safety and we want kids to be friends. We do *not* want them to form cliques or isolated groups and stay there. So, the prerogative of the game leader is to mix things up and challenge internal groups to get out of their cliques and mix and mingle with others. This is because we *know* there are *more* potential friendships out there waiting to be discovered, and we *know* that it is good and right and developmentally sound for children to know how to interact with a variety of people and personalities and to have the confidence to be themselves. Working toward building those competencies and skills starts with intentionally mixing things up from time to time—just to keep it interesting.

GAMES AS MIXERS

TIME
5 minutes

THE GAME Call out a random way to group players together. As quickly as possible, they should form a circle so that they are standing in order according to that grouping. For instance, if you called out that they should circle up according to height, the tallest player would be adjacent to the next tallest and so on, around the circle to the shortest player in the group. In some cases, you can add to the challenge by having them do this circling-up activity silently. After participants are circled up, break them into smaller groups wherever you wish by counting off—the first five go here, the second five make up the next team, and so on.

Sample circle-ups:

Middle name (alphabetically)

Birthday

Number of siblings (if they have the same number, choose who's first in line in the circle by the sibling that's the oldest)

Number of pets (they can break a tie by determining which pets are larger)

Shoe size (they can break a tie by choosing the most colorful shoes)

Number of cities lived in

ASSET CATEGORIES: Support, Social Competencies, Positive Identity

Players in the Band

TIME
5 minutes

SUPPLIES

- Index cards (one card per player)
- Pens

PREP On each index card, write down an instrument name. Make four identical cards for each instrument name (drum, guitar, piano, harp, flute, trumpet, saxophone, harmonica).

THE GAME Give a musical card to each player. Players should find their partners by pretending to play their instrument and making that instrument's sound, but they cannot talk to each other. (For example, flute players will hold their hands in a flutelike position and make a whistling sound to represent a flute.) If your group is made up of younger children, feel free to demonstrate or show an example of how to pretend to play the instruments.

You could also play a variation of this game in which players try to assemble a band with one of each kind of instrument.

ASSET CATEGORIES: Constructive Use of Time, Social Competencies

Singing Partners

TIME
5–10 minutes

SUPPLIES

- Index cards (one for each player)

PREP Write familiar song titles on the index cards. Make sure each song has at least two cards with its title on them.

Sample songs:
"The ABC Song"
"The Barney Song"
"B-I-N-G-O"
"Do Your Ears Hang Low?"
"Happy Birthday to You"
"Head and Shoulders Knees and Toes"

THE GAME Pass out index cards to players and tell them to keep their song assignments a secret. On your cue, all of the players should begin singing the song whose title is written on their cards and find the other players who are singing the same tune. Once they've found their partners, they can finish their songs with gusto. Beyond organizing the players into small partnerships or teams, this game can also be used as an icebreaker to energize the group as a whole.

ASSET CATEGORIES: Constructive Use of Time, Positive Values, Social Competencies

Lollipop Tongues Break Out

TIME
5 minutes

SUPPLIES

- Suckers, lollipops, or hard candies (one per person)

THE GAME Distribute the treats. Let players finish the treats. When you are ready to break the group into random teams, have each person stick out her or his tongue. Groups can now be formed by the different colors showing on the tips of their tongues!

ASSET CATEGORIES: Constructive Use of Time, Social Competencies

Circus Stars

TIME
5 minutes

SUPPLIES

- Index cards (one per person)

PREP On each of the cards, write or draw a circus role—trapeze artist, juggler, tightrope walker, magician, stunt rider, lion tamer, clown, and so on. There should be three to five cards with the same role.

THE GAME Shuffle the cards and distribute them randomly. Without talking, each player should pantomime her or his circus role in order to find all players with the same card. Once the circus teams have been assembled, have them stay together to work on the next activity.

ASSET CATEGORIES: Support, Empowerment, Constructive Use of Time

Choice Picks

TIME
5 minutes

THE GAME Have everyone stand. Explain that you will call out four choices and players must choose which one best describes their preference. Then they will go stand in the part of the room that you point to that represents that particular choice. For example, you might say "cake" (and point to the left side of the room), "cookies" (and point to the right side of the room), "ice cream" (point straight in front of you), and "candy" (point behind you). Each player determines which choice is her or his preference, and then goes to stand wherever you designated for that item. If four groups are all you need, you can stop here or repeat a few more sorting categories to let the group move and discover the various things they have in common with others (sample categories: Super Bowl/World Cup/World Series/Final Four, jazz/hip-hop/country/rock, folding laundry/dusting/picking up/washing dishes).

However, if you need to sort the four groups further, have them stay in the area of the room where they are with their "like interest" friends from the first sorting. Now call out new categories to sort by *within* their smaller groups, such as "cat person" or "dog person." This will further divide your group from four groups into eight. If any particular group is lopsided, call out more divisions until you get fairly evenly distributed groups (examples: board games/relay races, movie/book, pizza/hamburgers, spring/fall).

ASSET CATEGORIES: Constructive Use of Time, Social Competencies, Positive Identity

Rhyming Partners

TIME
10 minutes

SUPPLIES
- Index cards (at least one per player)

PREP Create sets of rhyming word cards (at least one card per player), writing each word of the rhyming pair on a different card. For example, write *song* on one card and its rhyming match *long* on another card. Other examples: *rock* and *sock*, *hop* and *bop*, *silly* and *Willy*, and *game* and *tame*.

THE GAME Shuffle the cards and give everyone one card each. When you give the cue, ask participants to hunt for their rhyming word partners. When each player finds her or his partner, the partners should all stand together in a large circle. Go to each pair and let them announce their rhyming words.

NOTE This game works especially well in a large group (more than 20), as it presents an appropriate challenge when players try to find their partners.

ASSET CATEGORIES: Constructive Use of Time, Commitment to Learning, Social Competencies

Friendship Starters

Whoever wants to understand much must play much.
—**GOTTFRIED BENN,** German essayist and poet

Once players are paired or grouped with other players, and they know names and have begun to relax a little, then an opportunity reveals itself, simply waiting to be maximized. By play development standards, this is the beginning of the second phase of group work: building relationships.

Whereas getting names down pat was the necessary first step, and mixing people up to encourage friendliness was a good second step, now is the time to start building real connections, to begin developing friendships.

Friendship starters move beyond mere names. These games help children begin to really get to know each other on a more personal level. Taking time to know someone says, "I like you. I'm interested in you. I know things about you. I know who you are and what makes you tick." When you start to know someone, you are taking essential steps toward building a relationship with that person. Consequently, you are also breaking down those individual scary feelings (yours and theirs) about who everyone is in the group and how well everyone is going to get along. You are helping them develop common ground.

The games in this chapter introduce and encourage friendship starters. They provide the play space for children to learn and practice friendship skills through conversation starters and games to develop social skills.

FUN STARTS

Connections

TIME
5–8 minutes

THE GAME Instruct players to mingle with as many people as they can in five minutes. They should exchange names and find something they have in common—things they like to eat, what they do for fun, whether or not they have pets, how many siblings they have, and so on. At the end of the allotted time, ask if they remember how many people they met. Determine who met the most people. Ask how many people can remember all the names of the people they met. Ask for volunteers to try to name each person they met *and* the thing they had in common with each one.

NOTE You can slow down the pace of meeting and making connections by adding in these instructions: "You must also shake hands and make eye contact with each person."

GOING DEEPER

- Did having a goal of finding things in common with others help you in your efforts for conversation? Why or why not?
- Is meeting others a skill that comes naturally to you?
- What makes it easier to meet others? What tips can you give each other?
- Does finding out that you have something in common with someone you just met make it easier to talk with that person? Why or why not?
- What can you take from this game to help you build friendships with others?

ASSET CATEGORIES: Support, Social Competencies, Positive Identity

Conversation Rotations

TIME

5–10 minutes

SUPPLIES

- Index cards (two per player)

PREP On each card, write an incomplete statement that players will use to talk about themselves. The following are examples of these statements:

I like neighbors who . . .

I like to play sports that . . .

I like to spend time with people who . . .

I like to go places that have . . .

I like to read books about . . .

I like spending time outside to . . .

I like to collect . . .

I like to play games that . . .

THE GAME Give each player two cards. On "Go," players should roam around the room, introducing themselves to each other (exchanging names and a handshake). In the third meeting, after introductions, they should turn over one of their cards, see what it says, and—taking turns—each should finish the statement on her card, and then politely ask the other player, "What about you?" The other player comments, then reads his statement and asks the first player, "What about you?" and allows that player to comment. When they are finished, they continue mingling until they've greeted two more people, and then they have a conversation with a sixth player. Keep people on the same pace by counting rounds out loud: "One. Two. Three. Shake hands. Share."

GOING DEEPER

- What did you learn about others from this game that you didn't know?
- What was difficult about this game?

- Did everyone look each other in the eye when they exchanged greetings? Did you shake hands? Exchange names?

- Why do you think those things are important to do when you are meeting new people?

- How does it feel to do all those actions?

- What message do you think it sends to others when you are able to meet and greet them well?

ASSET CATEGORIES: Support, Social Competencies

Lucky Numbers

TIME
10 minutes

THE GAME Make sure your group has space to move around. Divide the players into pairs, trying to partner children who don't often work or play together. Each person should silently think of a number between one and nine, and then share the number with her or his partner. Tell players they will be using their numbers to respond to a series of tasks. It will be easiest to explain each task individually before beginning that particular step.

1. In pairs, share the two numbers. Take the larger number. Both partners should share that many random facts about themselves. For example, if the largest number in a pair were nine, a player would share nine personal facts: "I like to paint, I play goalie, my favorite food is fried chicken . . . ," and so on.

2. Players should determine the smaller number in their pair and find that many things they have in common.

3. Next, the partners should add the smaller number and the larger number together. Both players should cross their arms, with their hands resting on top of their elbows and circle around each other in a do-si-do as many times as their combined number.

4. The pair should subtract the smallest number from the largest number and do that many double skips around the room (link elbows and skip together).

GOING DEEPER

- What did you and your partner learn about each other?

- What's one thing you want to ask your partner more about?

- What did you notice about the pairs around the room? Did you see people laughing and being silly with people that they don't usually hang out with?

- It's easy to get "stuck in a rut" with our friends, always playing with the same people over and over again. Why is it important to do things with new people sometimes?

- Do you want to be known as someone who excludes "outsiders," or as someone who welcomes new people into your group?

- Silently think of one new person you'd like to reach out to this week. It might be someone in your group of children, or someone on your basketball team, or someone in your scout troop, but pick one person you can spend time with this week. Make a promise to yourself to try to get to know that person better.

ASSET CATEGORIES: Support, Commitment to Learning, Social Competencies, Positive Identity

Categorically Speaking

TIME
10–30 minutes

SUPPLIES

- Paper and pens

THE GAME Split players into small groups of six to eight, and provide each group with paper and a pen. There are four rounds to this game.

1. *Animals*. Ask the groups to take two minutes to list as many things as possible that all of them have in common under this category. For example, have they all had pets? Have they all been to a zoo?

Have they all watched the Animal Planet channel? Encourage them to think creatively. When time is up, have groups count the number of things they have in common and write down the total number on their paper.

2. Players should repeat the process from round 1, but find what they have in common based on the category of *Creative Activities*.

3. Players should repeat the process from round 2, but find what they have in common based on the category of *free time*.

4. Let players name things they have in common that haven't already been mentioned.

Have each group tally the total number of commonalities that their group found.

Other example categories: music, vacation, family.

GOING DEEPER

- Did you find you had more in common than you thought you might? Why or why not?

- What kinds of things did you discover you had in common in the fourth round, when you were left to yourselves with no category to guide the conversation?

- Was it difficult to find things in common without having a particular thing to focus on?

- Starting a conversation is an important friendship skill. How do you start conversations with new people that you meet?

- How can discovering things you have in common with others lead to new friendships and stronger friendships?

ASSET CATEGORIES : Support, Social Competencies, Positive Identity

Color Hunt

TIME

10–12 minutes

SUPPLIES

- A color card (see the Prep section) and pencil for each player

PREP On a sheet of paper, list various colors in a grid:

Tan	Dark green	Light green	Purple
Yellow	Navy blue	Light blue	Pink
Brown	Peach	Black	Orange
Gold	Silver	Gray	Yellow orange
Lavender	Red	Orange red	Yellow green

THE GAME Give each person a color card and a pencil. Explain that players have five minutes to find and match as many individual colors on the card as possible to one other person who is wearing something that is that exact color. When they spot a color, they should go to the person wearing that color, introduce themselves, and ask the color wearer to sign her or his first name inside the color square. Each person can sign each card only one time, so that a complete color card should have 16 different signatures. (If your group has fewer than 16 people, either cross out some of the colors on the list, or allow people to sign each card two times.)

After five minutes, call time, and circle up to debrief the activity. Players do not necessarily need to find every color or fill up their color cards for the game to be successful—the goal of this game is to meet and interact with others.

GOING DEEPER

- Were you able to fill out your whole color card?
- Did you meet anyone new through this activity? Or did you talk with someone you don't usually talk to?

- Why is it important to make it a point to talk with new people, instead of only talking with your little circle of friends?

- Think of someone in the group that you would like to get to know better this week.

- This game gave you a reason to talk to many different people, even people you didn't know very well. What about in real life, when you see someone you don't know? How might you start a conversation with that person, or invite her or him to hang out with your friends?

- Why is it important to take the initiative to reach out to new people?

ASSET CATEGORIES: Support, Boundaries and Expectations, Social Competencies

Snowball Conversations

TIME
5–12 minutes

SUPPLIES

- Paper and a pencil for each participant

THE GAME Have every player write down her or his name and favorite book (or favorite hobby, food, subject in school, sport, thing to do on the weekend, place to visit, etc.) on a sheet of paper—the topic can be your choice. Divide the group into small teams of four to six, and have the teams cluster in separate areas. Ask them to wad up their papers and toss them on the floor in their little circle. These wads of paper are to be considered "snowballs" in this game. Shuffle the paper wads a little bit. On "Go," each player picks up a snowball and finds the player whose name is on the paper; these "Snowball Partners" exchange greetings and ask one another to say a little bit about the favorite that is listed.

Here's the tricky part. As two players start a conversation, other players may come up since they're trying to find their Snowball Partner. When the new player finds two already engaged in conversation, whoever is speaking should finish talking about her or his favorite, and then the other player should turn to the player who made the approach and welcome that person. For example, Stephanie might say something like, "Hello, Desiree. Jackson was just telling me about . . ." and then make a few comments about what she and Jackson had been discussing, followed by "Would you like to join us?"

The players are practicing making introductions, engaging in conversation, and making others feel welcome when they join in.

GOING DEEPER

- Did you have to approach two people who were already in conversation? How did you let them know you were there without being rude or interrupting?

- If you were already in conversation, how did you adjust to make the new person feel welcome?

- What strategies can we take from this game that we can use to include others? How can we interrupt conversations in a friendly way?

- What did you learn about the favorite things of people in our group? Would you be willing to share one of the conversations you had with your Snowball Partners?

- What do you do when you need to interrupt an adult who is talking? How do you decide if it's okay to interrupt?

- What about if we're in a big group? How can we make sure that all of the group members, from the quietest to the most vocal, have "space" to share their opinions and feel like the group has heard them?

ASSET CATEGORIES: Support, Empowerment, Boundaries and Expectations, Commitment to Learning, Positive Values, Social Competencies, Positive Identity

Elbow Tag

TIME
10–15 minutes

THE GAME Give players time to think about their favorite color, candy bar, ice cream flavor, and vegetable. Tell them to keep those favorites in mind for the remainder of the game. Designate a player to be "it" and a player to be the walker. Make sure "it" knows the walker she is chasing. "It" tries to tag the walker; the walker tries not to get tagged. Let other players, in pairs, link arms at the elbows and move to wherever they want to be in the designated playing area and stay still in that spot.

"It" yells out one of the categories of favorites. The walker goes to a pair and names his favorite from that category to the players he approaches. If his favorite is also a favorite of one of the players in the pair, then he links arms with the player who shares that favorite and the other player takes off as the new walker. If no one in the pair shares that favorite, then the walker continues on to a new pair, trying not to get tagged. "It" can change the category of favorite whenever she wants by yelling out the new category so that the walker can hear. If a walker is tagged, he becomes the new "it." For larger groups, it may be best to have two "its" and two walkers.

NOTE Players should not change their "favorites" in the middle of the game, deciding suddenly that their favorite vegetable is cauliflower, just because they need to match with one of the linked pairs.

GOING DEEPER

- When you were "the walker," how did you decide which linked pair to approach for safety?

- In the game, were you ever linked with a partner you didn't know very well? If you had favorites in common, how did that feel?

- This game balanced being active and talking. How important is it to balance physical activity (running, playing, jumping around) and quieter activities like talking with others?

- When you are on your own on the playground, in the cafeteria, or somewhere else, how do you decide on a "safe" group of people to hang out with?

- Sometimes people appear to be very different—they look different, they dress differently, they are in different grades. But they probably also have things in common with you. Have you ever been surprised to discover that someone who seemed different from you actually had something in common with you?

- Here's your challenge for the week: find something that you have in common with someone that you think is very different from you.

ASSET CATEGORIES: Support, Constructive Use of Time, Commitment to Learning, Social Competencies

Loopy Conversations

TIME
10–15 minutes

SUPPLIES

- Colored cereal (Froot Loops, for example)
- Paper and pencils

PREP List the following questions on a sheet of paper (including the names of the colors), and make sure there are enough copies for each group of three or four players.

- Purple: What is your favorite thing to do on Saturdays?
- Red: If you could plan the perfect day, what would that day look like?
- Orange: What is a chore you don't mind doing to help out at home?
- Yellow: What makes you laugh?
- Green: Who do you like to spend time with?

THE GAME Have everyone get into small groups of three or four participants. First, they should share their names. Give each player a small handful of colored cereal, and give each team a sheet of questions. Tell everyone not to eat the cereal yet. Have players separate the cereal pieces in their hands by color. They should each pick out the color that is their favorite and answer the question related to that color as listed on the paper. They can then eat all their cereal of that color. Go around the circle. On the second round, have the others in the circle pick out a color for each player to answer a color-related question (then they can eat that color of their remaining cereal pieces). Keep going around the circle until all the cereal is eaten and all the color questions are explored.

NOTE This game could be adapted to use other types of items instead of food. For instance, players could answer questions based on items such as colored crayons, marbles, or dominoes.

GOING DEEPER

- Why is it important to laugh and have fun? To have friends with whom you like to spend time?

- What is a trait you look for in friends?

- What is a trait that makes you a good friend?

- Why is it important to help others?

- With the color red, you talked about doing whatever you wanted. That, in part, is about likes and goals. What is a goal you have for yourself?

- How can having conversations like these deepen your friendships and/or help you make new friends?

ASSET CATEGORIES: Support, Empowerment, Commitment to Learning, Social Competencies, Positive Identity

Design Your Own Superhero Identity

TIME
10–15 minutes

SUPPLIES

- Paper and a pencil for each player

THE GAME Tell participants that they each have superhero potential and qualities. Each player should take two minutes to design her or his own personal superhero identity using pencil and paper. The superheroes should represent some of the players' real traits (being kind to animals, helping others, being respectful) as well as some superhuman traits they would like to have (flying, having X-ray vision, crawling up walls, leaping tall buildings).

When time is up, players should form teams of three to share their superhero selves with each other—their names, their best traits, and the superhuman traits they wish to have. Give them five minutes to share.

For additional fun, have the three superheroes come up with a title and description for a movie or comic book they would star in together. Have superhero teams share their titles and set aside their work for more fun later (such as role playing, making videos, drawing comic-book cover designs, etc.).

GOING DEEPER

- What's cool about being a superhero?
- What traits do your fellow group members have that make them super?
- What traits did you hear other people say they have that they would also like to develop as part of their own superhero identities?
- What can you do to strengthen your super character?
- What can each person do to make this group a superhero team?
- Who are the superheroes in your life that mean a lot to you? What do they do that makes them so special to you?

ASSET CATEGORIES: Support, Commitment to Learning, Positive Values, Positive Identity

Names Stack

This game is recommended for grades 2 and up.

TIME
5–8 minutes

SUPPLIES

- Paper and pen for each team of four to six people

THE GAME Divide the group into teams of four to six players. Make sure that each team has paper to write on. Have each team write their first names on their paper in a vertical list.

Example:

> Susan
>
> George
>
> Ricky
>
> Cassandra

Give teams two minutes to create as many words as they can from the letters in their names. For example, the name list above might generate words such as *sack, rake, car, gorge* . . . The letters do not have to "touch" to make a word. Each letter can be used only once within a single word, but teams can use each letter multiple times to make as many words as they possibly can. The team with the most words wins.

GOING DEEPER

- What's the best word your team came up with?
- If you were working alone with these names, do you think you would have found more words or fewer words?
- How well did you work together as a team?
- Name some other situations where we need others to help us.
- What are some things that you learned in this game? Did you learn teammates' names, how to spell words, or how to rearrange words in your head?
- This game made learning fun. What are other ways you can make learning about someone or something fun?

ASSET CATEGORIES: Support, Empowerment, Commitment to Learning

TIME
10–15 minutes

SUPPLIES

- Paper strips and pencils
- Paper bag for collecting paper strips

THE GAME Distribute paper strips to all players. Ask them to write down one name on the piece of paper—it can be the name of someone in the room, a favorite cartoon person, a superhero, a favorite teacher, or someone famous. Tell them to try to name someone whom at least three other people in the room would know. Collect all the strips.

Divide the group into smaller teams of six to eight. Have a representative from the first team come up, draw a name, and give clues to the other teams about the identity of the person on the strip. For example, if the name is Snoopy, the clue giver might say, "Charlie Brown is his friend. He fights the Red Baron and hangs out with Woodstock." If players draw a paper strip with the name of another person in the room, they could point or nod their head in that individual's direction, or get as creative as they want to. Allow the clue giver 20–30 seconds to give clues. If any of the teams guess correctly, they get a point, and the clue-giving team also gets a point for its descriptive skills. Continue play, rotating among the teams.

NOTE Clue givers are simply trying to rack up points for their team by being the best clue givers. When their turn is up, all teams get a chance to guess.

GOING DEEPER

- What, if anything, was frustrating about this game?

- In this game, you had clues to help you guess who was being described. Clues are signals. What signals tell you if someone is friendly or not? How do you know if you can go up and start a conversation with that person?

- What signal do we send to show others that we are friendly and nice?

- Talk about the names that were listed. Why did you pick the people you did?

- What did you learn about your teammates in this activity?

- How can you use people's strengths when you are working together on future activities?

ASSET CATEGORIES: Support, Empowerment, Social Competencies, Positive Identity

Just Roll It

TIME
10–20 minutes

SUPPLIES

- Six-sided die

THE GAME Go around the circle and have each player roll the die and respond to the statement that corresponds to the number rolled, as follows:

One: one thing you like to do with your family

Two: one thing you are trying to learn how to do better

Three: one book that you think every child should read

Four: the superhero character you think is most like *you*

Five: one fun thing to do in your city

Six: one way you make each day a great day

If time allows, go around the circle as many times as desired.

GOING DEEPER

- Now that we've shared favorites, what is one thing you'd like to try?

- What are some things we talked about today that make us proud?

- All the answers you shared are things and people that you value, cherish, and feel are important and special. How can you show others that you value them?

- Now let's flip it around: *you* are valuable. What are the things that make you valuable?

- It's easy to respect and value people you like, but what about people you don't like? Is it still important to respect and value them? Why or why not?

- How can we continue to value the uniqueness of everyone in our group, including ourselves?

ASSET CATEGORIES: Support, Empowerment, Constructive Use of Time, Commitment to Learning, Positive Values, Positive Identity

Star Inquirer

TIME

15 minutes

SUPPLIES

- Paper and a pen for each team of four

THE GAME Divide the group into teams of four players each, and have the groups move to different parts of the room. Each group should pick one player to be its Star. The others on the team will take five minutes to ask their Star questions. They will write down five things they found most interesting about their Star for the *Star Inquirer*. For example, *This person started singing in musicals when she was four*; or, *This Star can name and describe 30 types of dinosaurs*; or, *This Star hopes to be a children's book illustrator one day*.

When time is up, choose one group to go first and have a representative from that group (other than the Star) read the list of facts about its Star, as reported to the *Star Inquirer*. The other teams will each get one guess as to who they think the Star in the group is, based on the facts read aloud. Acknowledge each team that guesses correctly. Rotate to the next team and repeat the process.

GOING DEEPER

- How did it feel to hear the things other people thought were "cool" about you?
- How did you decide what facts you wanted to know about your Star?
- What did you learn about each other from this game?
- How can you take more time to really get to know others?
- Why is it so powerful when we are known and liked?
- How does that knowledge affect the way you act?

ASSET CATEGORIES: Support, Empowerment, Commitment to Learning, Social Competencies, Positive Identity

Shuffle the Deck

TIME

5–10 minutes

SUPPLIES

- Deck of standard playing cards

THE GAME Distribute one card to each player. Call out a random grouping of cards and have players find their teammates. For example, "Find three of you: three 4s, three kings, three 10s," and so on. Once players are in their groups, give each group a question or topic to chat about for a minute after introductions are made. Call out as many combinations as you want. If you have a small group, you can distribute two cards to each person, or you can take out all cards aces through fives.

Sample groupings:

- Find six other numbers the same *color* as you (red, black).
- Find eight other numbers in the same *suit* as you (spades, hearts, clubs, diamonds).
- Get with three other people so that you make up four numbers in a row (for example, 6, 7, 8, 9 or 10, jack, queen, king).
- Create a group whose numbers add up to 12.
- Create a group whose numbers add up to 25.
- Find all the other numbers just like you.
- Create a group of three—anyone.
- Create a group of four—all odds or all evens.
- Create a group of all royal face cards.

Sample questions:

- Talk about a book you read and loved.
- Say what your favorite food is.
- Talk about your best friend and why you like her or him.
- Talk about your favorite subject in school.

- Talk about a way you can help other people.
- Talk about a pet you have or would like to have.

NOTE Be sure to distribute the face cards (the king, queen, and jack) so that you can ask the questions that match them in the Going Deeper section. Make sure the combinations you call work out to include the number of people you have, *or* be ready to handle players who aren't matched into a group (for example, if one person is left over, have him or her join another group, or have those whose cards are not called create their own random group).

GOING DEEPER

- What other questions could we have asked to find out more about each other?
- You were put together with others in many different groups. Why is it important to be able to mingle and mix with different groups? What can we learn by being kind and friendly to everyone we meet?
- One of the ways we got into a group was by creating a "royal family." What is one thing that makes your family special?
- Members of royal families carry themselves with dignity. How do you carry yourself with pride? What other qualities make up "royal" character?
- If our group was compared to the cards, then who among us has a big heart? Who in the group is the joker and makes everyone laugh? Who is willing to dig in and do the hard or dirty work (spade)? Who "sparkles" and makes us happy to be part of our group?
- How can we use the unique strengths of various people in our group to be a better team?

ASSET CATEGORIES: Support, Empowerment, Positive Values, Social Competencies, Positive Identity

Guardian Shields

TIME
15 minutes

SUPPLIES

- One writing utensil and one copy of a drawing of a shield per player

PREP Draw a simple shield, divided into six parts or boxes.

THE GAME For five minutes, each player should decorate a shield, depicting a personal strength in each of the six segments:

1. Write your name.
2. Draw a symbol that defines you, such as a heart, a smiley face, a trophy, or a common shape.
3. Draw something about yourself that makes you proud.
4. Draw an adult who is always supportive of you.
5. Draw a friend who helps you make smart choices.
6. Draw something that keeps you strong and healthy.

Organize the players into smaller table groups and let them share their shields when time is up. Let people choose one or two parts of their shield to share with the large group. Post the shield drawings on the wall to remind participants of their personal strengths.

GOING DEEPER

- What's one thing you realized about yourself through this activity?
- What's one cool thing you learned about another person?
- Who are the people that help you be your best?
- What are the things in your life that make you stronger?
- Shields protect people. How do the things on your shield protect you?
- What is one thing you can do to protect yourself from harm?

ASSET CATEGORIES: Support, Empowerment, Constructive Use of Time, Positive Identity

Connect Four

TIME
5–10 minutes

THE GAME Encourage players to mingle around the room, smiling and greeting each other. When you call "Connect," each individual should link arms with one other player. Give pairs 30 seconds to find one thing they have in common with each other. Then have them unlink and start mingling again, each finding new players to link with.

Continue the process of mingle, connect, share, mingle, connect, share for several rounds. At some point after a pair has linked and shared things they have in common, yell out "Connect four!" Pairs should stay linked and scramble to "connect four" (two pairs linked together by one player from each team joining arms). Give them 20 seconds. The two players who join together to "connect four"—forming the new link—must find something that they have in common.

Once time is up, yell "Connect eight!" The players who form new links between the two groups of four now must find something they have in common. Continue creating as big a connected chain of players as desired. When you're ready to stop play, have the players stay linked, then go through each chain, and ask the connected players to share what they have in common, link by link.

This game can also be played as a mixer to form new small groups for other activities.

NOTE If there is an odd number of players, ask one of the adult helpers to play, or ask one of the young people to help you make the "calls."

GOING DEEPER

- What kinds of connections did you make during this game?
- What kinds of things did you talk about in order to discover what you had in common?
- What did you learn about other people?
- At the end, we were all connected by different links along the way and created a huge human chain. What are some things you think all of us have in common?

- How can we use what we learned in this game to reach out and become friends with others, even with those who may or may not look like us or who on first glance don't seem to have anything in common with us?

ASSET CATEGORIES: Support, Social Competencies

Fingers Down

TIME
15 minutes

THE GAME Gather the group to sit in a circle. All players should hold out their hands in front of them, palms facing outward, with their fingers pointing up in the air (think of a two-handed stop sign movement, as a police officer might use to control traffic). Start play by saying to everyone, "Fingers down if you have gone hiking in another state," or you can choose some other activity. Players who have done the stated activity (hiking in another state) should fold one of their pinky fingers down, so nine fingers are left pointing to the sky.

Play proceeds clockwise, until every player has shared a statement. Every time a player has done the activity stated, he or she must fold down another finger, starting with the pinky, then the ring finger, then the middle finger, until he or she has worked through both hands and folded down all 10 fingers. The winners are the players who are able to keep at least one finger up the entire game after play has circled through the whole group one time. A clever player might choose to share an activity that most people have done, but he or she hasn't. Other example statements might include, "Fingers down if you have worn your pajamas out of the house," or "Fingers down if you have been camping," or "Fingers down if you can play a musical instrument."

GOING DEEPER

- Did you hear anything that made you think about something you would like to do?

- Did you think of other topics that would be fun to use in this game?

- This game is great practice for starting conversations with people, whether they are new friends, adults, or classmates. Did this game give you any ideas for things to talk about with people you don't know very well?

- Who do you know who's great at starting conversations and getting to know other people?

- What's one way you could get better about talking to people you don't know very well?

ASSET CATEGORIES: Support, Empowerment, Social Competencies, Positive Identity

Relationship Builders

It is play and only play that makes man complete.
—JOHANN FRIEDRICH VON SCHILLER, German poet and philosopher

Whether one is in a small group of friends or a big group of children, some powerful dynamics come into play, which can affect the quality of any relationship. It is wise for the leader of the group to introduce a healthy respect for these factors early on in the play development of a group. The sooner children embrace and accept the crazy dynamics that come with relationships and teams, the better off they'll be in working well with others for the long haul.

We recognize that there are many dimensions to relationships—many qualities, attributes, and differences. Every relationship is unique; it is unique to the people involved, unique to the circumstances from which it was birthed, and unique to the environment in which it developed. However, some elements seemingly influence relationships every time:

1. **The dynamics of interpersonal relationships.** This element is the way a group or even two people interact when they are together. It includes the group's norms, rules, and expectations (spoken or otherwise); the way group members work together; and even how welcoming they are to each other.

2. **Personality details.** This element takes into consideration the character, emotions, and quirkiness of the individual.

3. **Diversity appreciation.** This third influence can strengthen and enrich relationships by encouraging acceptance of what makes each of us unique and special in multiple ways, as well as appreciation of what we have in common.

These three elements can enhance or hurt any relationship. Our job is to provide opportunities for children to discover and develop an understanding and appreciation of these different aspects through play development that lets them build a healthy respect for themselves and others. The following games introduce these important relationship builders.

GROUP DYNAMICS

Buzzing Bee

TIME
5–15 minutes

SUPPLIES

- One quarter (or other large coin)

THE GAME Have players sit on the floor in a circle. Select one player to be the Beekeeper and leave the room. After the player has left the area, give the quarter, representing the "tasty honey," to one of the remaining players, who then becomes the Queen (or King) Bee. The Queen Bee should hide the quarter in her or his hands. All of the other players are bees, and all players in the room should put their hands behind their backs. The group's job is to make a buzzing sound to indicate to the Beekeeper when he or she is getting closer to the Queen Bee or farther away while the Beekeeper walks around inside the circle. The bees should be silent when the Beekeeper is far from the Queen Bee, and start to buzz more loudly as the Beekeeper gets closer. This is like the "hotter/colder" concept. The louder the buzzing, the closer the Beekeeper is to the Queen Bee. The buzzing will provide the clues to locating the Queen Bee and the honey.

When the bees are ready, have the Beekeeper return to the room and begin the game. The Beekeeper gets three guesses (or as many as you want) to name the Queen Bee and find the honey. Once the Queen Bee is discovered, choose the next Beekeeper and begin again with a new Queen Bee.

GOING DEEPER

- How easy was it for the Beekeeper to discover the Queen Bee?
- What is a goal that you have achieved as a group? How did you help each other reach that goal?
- In this game, we buzzed loudly when the Beekeeper was close to finding the Queen Bee providing encouragement. Who encourages you?

- What is something that you get excited about and "buzz" loudly over?

- Paying attention to clues is a key part of this game. There are also clues that help us in our friendships. What clues might tell us that a friend is sad? Lonely? Happy? Worried? Embarrassed? Proud? Frustrated? What might you do for your friend?

- How do you become a better friend by paying attention to clues and responding to your friends accordingly?

ASSET CATEGORIES: Support, Social Competencies, Positive Identity

Duck, Duck, Goose

TIME
5–15 minutes

THE GAME Have players sit on the floor in a circle. Select one player to be "it." "It" walks around the circle, tapping each player's head while saying, "Duck, Duck, Duck . . ." Eventually, "it" selects one player, taps her or his head, and yells "Goose!" The "Goose" then gets up and chases "it" around the circle and tries to tag her or him. If the Goose tags "it," then "it" remains "it." If "it" makes the trip all the way around the circle and is able to sit down in the space left vacant by the Goose without being tagged, then the Goose becomes the new "it." Play resumes.

GOING DEEPER You've probably all played this game before, but you might not have thought about all the lessons you can learn from it.

- The Duck, Goose, and "it" each have an important role. Why do you think we need different roles in a group?

- What was the advantage of being "it"? What about being the Goose?

- The Goose has a job it knows it has to do. What is a job that you know you have to do as a member of this group? At home? At school?

- There are times when "it" gets to decide what will happen. What is something you get to choose to do at home? At school? With friends?

- "It" chose the Ducks and Geese in this game. Whom do you pick to be your friends?
- What qualities and characteristics do you look for in a good friend?

ASSET CATEGORIES: Empowerment, Boundaries and Expectations, Social Competencies, Positive Identity

Balloon Cup Race

TIME
15–20 minutes

SUPPLIES
- Four empty 6- to 8-ounce cups
- 100 filled water balloons
- Four medium-size garbage cans (25 of the water balloons per can)

PREP Fill 100 balloons with water (we suggest using a spout or a funnel!). The amount of time to dedicate to this task will vary greatly. Enlisting help from others and using multiple water sources will be helpful.

THE GAME Since this game involves many water balloons, there is a good chance that players and the playing area may get wet. Playing outdoors is recommended.

First, divide the group into four teams of 5–15 players. Have teams line up in parallel lines, with three to five feet between each person on any given team. Give an empty cup to the player at the end of each line. At the front of each line, place the garbage cans filled with water balloons. On the count of three, the player at the front of each line (next to the garbage cans) grabs one water balloon and tosses it to the next player in line. The water balloon is tossed from player to player until it gets to the next-to-the-last person in line. That player pops the balloon and tries to get as much of the water as possible into the cup that is being held by the last person in line. Once the balloon has been popped, then the first player can grab the next water balloon and send it on its way. The team with the most water in its cup at the end wins. If the players struggle with popping the balloons, they can switch places with other players, or you could suggest that they try using a pen to puncture the balloons.

GOING DEEPER

- What was your reaction when you dropped a balloon? When you passed on a balloon? When you got wet? This part of the game is like life. Sometimes we drop things; sometimes we are right on target and do things well; sometimes we make mistakes. How would you like to be treated when you make a mistake?

- How kindly or thoughtfully do you treat others when they make mistakes? What rules should we set as a group to note how we all want to be treated when we make mistakes?

- In real life, when we drop things or make mistakes, we can learn and adjust to do better the next time. Can you think of a time when you made a mistake, learned from it, and did things differently the next time?

- What about a time when everything was just right and you did something really good, right on target? Are you proud of yourself in a good way or do you brag to others? How could you share your successes with others in a humble and unselfish way?

- What is something you want to improve and do better for yourself? How can you start to do that this week?

- What is something you would like to improve and do better as a group? How can we start today?

ASSET CATEGORIES: Support, Commitment to Learning, Social Competencies, Positive Identity

Cymbal Crashers

TIME
10–20 minutes

SUPPLIES

- Metal pan and large metal spoon, or a whistle

THE GAME As you use the spoon to hit the pan (representing a cymbal) a certain number of times players should listen for the number of crashes and quickly form small, tight circles of the specific number tapped out on the cymbal. For example, the first set of cymbal crashes might equal six, so players should form tight circles with six people. The next set of cymbal crashes might equal three, so players would create tight circles with three people each. Individuals who are unable to make a small group with the correct number of people will be "out" of the game. They will then sit on the sidelines. Continue beating out numbers until only two people, the winners, are remaining.

NOTE If a metal pan is not available, another option would be to blow a whistle or simply clap your hands in place of the cymbal crashes.

GOING DEEPER

- How did you find your small groups each time?
- How do you choose your friendship circles?
- How did it feel to include someone in a group? To exclude someone?
- How did it feel to be left out of a group? To be welcomed into a group?
- How can we make sure that our group is always welcoming to others?
- How might you design a community/school/club that welcomes all different kinds of people?

ASSET CATEGORIES: Support, Empowerment, Boundaries and Expectations, Social Competencies

Puzzle-Piece Pictures

TIME
10–12 minutes

SUPPLIES

- Jigsaw picture puzzles, divided into groups of two or three linked pieces
- Paper
- Markers or crayons

THE GAME Divide the group into teams of three to five players. Distribute two to three linked pieces of a picture puzzle to the teams. Ask, "What picture does the puzzle piece make?" Instruct each team to lay the puzzle pieces on a piece of paper and work together to complete the picture by drawing around them. Note that there is no "right" way to complete the pictures, and encourage players to use their imagination. After five minutes of drawing, let the groups cluster together at each piece of artwork so that the artists can tell the group about their masterpieces.

For additional fun (if time allows), have each group create a story around its puzzle pieces to go with the picture.

NOTE Remind participants to respect one another's artwork and presentations. Reinforce that it is never all right to laugh at another person or another person's work in a hurtful way.

GOING DEEPER

- How did your team work together to craft your final picture?
- If our group were a picture, what might it be? Why?
- How is our group like a puzzle with many pieces?
- Sometimes puzzles get broken and messed up, and sometimes the things we do or say can hurt members of our group. How do we sometimes hurt each other, whether accidentally or on purpose?
- What rules do you think should be in place to help hold us together as a group? To help us get along?

- What could we do if we all worked together?

ASSET CATEGORIES: Support, Empowerment, Boundaries and Expectations, Constructive Use of Time, Social Competencies

TIME
10–20 minutes

SUPPLIES
- Scanned picture
- Poster board
- Two pieces of cardboard
- Glue
- Crayons

PREP Print out a large picture of your group (or logo or mascot), glue it onto the poster board, and cut it into puzzle pieces (enough for one piece per player). Cut two pieces of cardboard to be slightly larger than the poster-board puzzle.

THE GAME Distribute one piece to each player, picture side down. Ask players to write or draw on the blank side of their puzzle piece a word or symbol to represent a quality they contribute to the group. For example, you might say, "I have a positive attitude" or "I enjoy helping people" or "I'm creative." After three or four minutes, let each player quickly present her or his puzzle piece to the group, then have the whole group assemble the puzzle on top of one of the puzzle boards. Put the other puzzle board on top of the puzzle, hold tightly, and slowly flip it over. Remove the top puzzle board and reveal the picture to the group.

NOTE It takes courage and vulnerability to share your strengths in front of a group. Remind players to listen to one another respectfully as they share the contributions they can make to the group.

GOING DEEPER

- How did it feel to go from random puzzle pieces to a final product?
- When you saw what was on the other side of the puzzle, what were your thoughts?

If you're using a picture of the logo or mascot, follow up with these questions:

- Have you ever thought about how you "fit" into the bigger picture of this agency/school/group? Have you ever made the connection between this place where you spend time and who you are and the skills you have?
- We shared how our talents contribute to this group. How does our group contribute to this agency/school? How do we use our skills and talents to make this place better?

If you're using a picture of the group, follow up with these questions:

- Now that you've heard everyone share, how could all the pieces (our contributions) "fit" together to make a difference?
- What are the natural connections we have as a group? What makes our group a really good team?

ASSET CATEGORIES: Support, Empowerment, Boundaries and Expectations, Positive Identity

Traffic Patrol

TIME
10 minutes

THE GAME Have the group make a circle, face to back, all facing toward the right. When you say "Green," the group starts moving quickly to the right (clockwise). When you call "Yellow," the group should slow down to a crawl. On the cue of "Red," the group should quickly stop. If you call "U-turn," everyone should do an about-face and move in the opposite direction (counterclockwise). The challenge is to see how smoothly and quickly the group can move together.

GOING DEEPER

- How well did everyone do in following the traffic signals?

- What traffic signals do we have for us as a group? What are "red" signals—the things we shouldn't do? What are the "green" signals—the things that our group can and should do?

- When should we have "yellows" for our group? What calls for a "slowdown"?

- How well do we follow those signals as a group?

- Where can we improve?

- Think about your life. Have you ever had to do a quick U-turn because you realized you were going the wrong way? What happened? What helped you get going in the right direction?

ASSET CATEGORIES: Boundaries and Expectations, Positive Values, Social Competencies

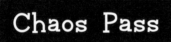

TIME 5–12 minutes

SUPPLIES

- Various objects, one per person: shoes, combs, balloons, tennis balls, Q-tips, paper, and so forth

THE GAME Give each person an object to hold. Organize players into groups of 10–12, and have the groups stand in circles. Tell them that they're going to create a little chaos and see how well they handle the pressure. On "Go," each player should pass the object he or she is holding to the person on the right *and* also receive the object the person on the left is passing. The goal is to keep all the objects moving without dropping any of them. Should anyone drop an object, he or she is out (as well as the object the person was holding). Keep playing until there is only one person left.

Ready for the next level? Round up the players. The same rules apply, except this time there's one teensy adjustment. When a player is out, her or his object remains *in* play. This adds to the chaos and challenge of keeping things going without being the one to drop anything.

GOING DEEPER

- With the level of excitement, did you pick up the speed in passing things or try to slow things down so that everyone had time to pass and receive?
- When your schedule gets crazy (homework, sports, faith community, etc.), how do you respond to the chaos?
- Do you slow things down to take naps or rest, drink water, and eat?
- What do you do to make sure you have enough energy and a good attitude to handle all your schoolwork and chores at home?

For older children:

- When you are studying for a hard test or memorizing information, it's easy to get overwhelmed with information. What tricks help you stay focused on studying and memorizing?

For pre-readers and early readers:

- When you are trying to read, it's easy to get overwhelmed with all the new words—just like having so many objects to juggle was overwhelming in this game. What do you do when you see words that you don't know? How do you feel when you read a hard page or finish a whole book?

ASSET CATEGORIES: Support, Constructive Use of Time, Commitment to Learning, Social Competencies, Positive Identity

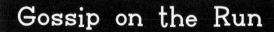

Gossip on the Run

TIME
10 minutes

SUPPLIES

- One piece of paper with a message consisting of about two or three sentences written on it

THE GAME Play a spin-off of the old gossip/telephone game. Have players form two lines facing each other. Show the player at one end of one of the lines the message you've crafted. (For pre-readers, you can whisper the message to them.) That person then runs across the space to the first person at the head of the other line and whispers the message into her ear and then returns to his original spot. The receiving player runs across the space to the next person in the line across from her and whispers the message into his ear. Players run back and forth across the space whispering their message until it reaches the end. The last "receiver" says the message out loud, and it is compared to the original written message.

Want to cross wires? Give the same message to a player from each side at opposite ends of the line (one player from one line and one end of the line and another player from the other line at the opposite end of the line) and have them run back and forth to other players. Compare messages received from the last two receivers to the original and see which version is close to correct.

GOING DEEPER

- Have you ever gotten the wrong message about someone else? (For example, you may have heard that someone is snobby, when really he or she is just shy.)

- How can you try to prevent getting the wrong message about another person again?

- Have you ever gotten the wrong message about something you were asked to do? (For example, have you ever thought you were supposed to meet your mom at 2:00, but she expected you to be there by 1:45?)

- How can you make sure the misunderstanding doesn't happen again?

- Have you ever deliberately given a wrong message about someone else? Did your choice have any consequences for you, for that person, or for anyone else?

- What is a strategy we can adopt to make sure we receive and give good information about others? (For example, don't gossip, make sure what we hear is correct by asking the person about it, etc.)

ASSET CATEGORIES: Support, Boundaries and Expectations, Positive Values, Social Competencies

Balloon Ups and Downs

TIME
5–10 minutes

SUPPLIES

- One balloon per person, plus a few extras in case one pops

PREP This activity might be too challenging for kindergartners if they can't blow up a balloon. Check with a few of the children beforehand to see if they are ready for this game.

THE GAME Have each person blow up a balloon, pinch it closed, and hold on to it without tying it. Stand in a circle so participants can see one another as they respond to the questions.

Think of a goal you have. It might be to score a point in the basketball game, or ace your spelling test, or save money to buy a new toy.

Let a little air out of the balloon if someone has put down your goal.

Let a little air out if someone has laughed at your goal.

Let a little air out if someone has distracted you from your goal.

Let a little air out if you have made choices that fought against your goal.

Let the balloons go. This symbolizes letting go of all the bad stuff so that we can focus on the good stuff.

GOING DEEPER

- What are some of the goals you were thinking about?
- Did you ever think about how many different things fight against your goals?

THE GAME, PART TWO Give each person a new balloon, and let players puff into their balloons after they answer the following questions out loud with a partner. After each puff, pinch the balloons closed to contain the air.

- What keeps you headed strongly toward your goals?
- Who are the people who support you in your goals?
- What is one way in which you stay focused on your goal?

- Share a time when you made good choices that helped you work toward your goal.

OPTION After a few minutes, have the participants fully inflate their balloons. Tie the balloons and tape them around the room in celebration of the group striving toward its goals.

GOING DEEPER, PART TWO

- What are some of the things you shared with your partners?
- How can we make sure we don't put down or laugh at the goals of others?
- How can we support one another in working toward our goals?

ASSET CATEGORIES: Support, Boundaries and Expectations, Social Competencies, Positive Identity

What's in a Look?

TIME
5–10 minutes

THE GAME Have the group circle up. Designate the starting leader. The leader should make a face of his choice (silly, serious, happy, confused) and turn to the player on the left. That player should mimic the look of the leader for all to see, then change that look to a facial expression of her choice and pass it on to the person on the left. The mimicking and creating of various facial expressions continue around the circle back to the leader.

GOING DEEPER

- Who had the funniest facial expression? The scariest? The nicest?

- What can our facial expressions, our "look," say about us?

- When people look at us, what do we want them to see?

- What could a smile do if we wore it all day? What could it do for us? What could it do for others?

- In this game, it was easy to change from a sad look to a happy look or a funny face to a scary face. In real life, how easy is it for us to change our moods (for instance, to go from sad to happy)?

- Sometimes someone else may give us a not-so-nice look. What can we do in those situations to not let the look bother us or change our good day?

ASSET CATEGORIES: Support, Social Competencies, Positive Identity

Extreme Teams

SUPPLIES

- Bubble gum (one piece per team of four to six)

THE GAME Divide the group into teams of four to six. (You could make up teams that have the maximum number of categories called, and have each player go once.) Players should rotate who participates in each round so that each round is covered by a different participant. Briefly read aloud all the categories. Let the teams have a few minutes to talk over who will take each category. Begin play. Call out a category. After it is called, each team should send up a representative. Judge the round, determine the winner, and award a point to the winning team for that round. Keep track of points and determine the "winners" of the game.

Sample categories:

The Silliest Laugh

Sings "Happy Birthday" the Fastest

The Fastest Snake Crawl

The Most Accurate Cartoon Imitation

Can Blow the Biggest Bubble

The Funniest Joke

The Highest Jump

GOING DEEPER

- This game points out different gifts or skills. We all have them. How often do you look for gifts, skills, or qualities you admire in others? Why is it important to point out the good qualities others have?

- What is one skill or talent you have that you are particularly proud of?

- What is a skill or talent you would like to learn?

- How could you use your skills or talents at home? At school? With your friends?

- How can we use all of our gifts and talents within this group? What is something we could do as a team?

Star Songs

TIME
15–20 minutes

SUPPLIES
- Paper
- Pencils

THE GAME Each person should write down two words that describe stellar or outstanding character. Divide the group into teams of four to six players, and ask each team to write a song using all the character words from its members' individual work. (Give them 5–10 minutes.) When time is up, have each team sing its song together for the rest of the group.

NOTE To save time, give the groups a familiar song, such as "Happy Birthday" or "Twinkle, Twinkle, Little Star," so they can use the tune they know as the base for their new lyrics.

GOING DEEPER
- Which song did you like best? Why?
- What did you think of the process of creating a song? What was it like?
- What was the hardest part of this activity?
- How does your own character measure up to the stellar character you described?
- How can you reach for the stars to have a more stellar character yourself? What is one action you can take this week?

- How can your group as a whole work to be a group of stellar character?

ASSET CATEGORIES: Support, Empowerment, Constructive Use of Time, Positive Values, Social Competencies

Hot Spot

TIME
10–15 minutes

SUPPLIES
- One chair per person
- Music (or someone who is willing to hum tunes)
- A bag of premade questions, cut into strips

PREP On paper strips, write the following questions:

What's one way you calm down when you're angry?

What's your favorite way to relax if you are worried?

What's your favorite way to study for a hard test?

What's your favorite sport to play, and why?

What is something that makes you mad easily?

What is one thing you can do if someone is trying to make you do something you know is wrong?

What is one way you can deal with gossip?

THE GAME Set chairs in a circle. Label one chair as the Hot Spot, and place a bag of questions under it. Start the music and let everyone walk clockwise around the circle. When the music stops, each person should quickly sit down in the closest chair. The person who lands in the Hot Spot should draw a question from the bag, read the question aloud, and answer it for the group.

GOING DEEPER

- In this game, you were in the Hot Spot. Some of the questions dealt with being in "hot" situations. How do you feel you dealt with being on the Hot Spot for the game? Was it scary? Fun? Easy?

- What is one thing that you want to try, after hearing a suggestion from your teammates? What's another question you think the group should answer?

- We just learned some things from each other. Friendships are powerful things. You are always learning from your friends, learning attitudes, skills, and ideas. What are some good things you are learning from your current group of friends?

- What are some negative things you might learn from friends? How can you combat those negative things by being a positive influence?

- It's important to choose friends wisely, because they have a huge impact on *you*. What are some things you should look for in a good friend?

- How can you build strong relationships with the friends you choose? How can you be a good friend?

If group energy is high, you could play the game again with your new questions.

ASSET CATEGORIES: Support, Empowerment, Boundaries and Expectations, Constructive Use of Time, Positive Values, Social Competencies

Static Relay

TIME
10–15 minutes

SUPPLIES

- Small five- to six-inch balloons (at least one per team—have extras in case some break)

- Masking tape

PREP Blow up a balloon for each group, plus a few extras. Mark two lines that are approximately 20 feet apart.

THE GAME Divide the group into two teams of 8–10 players each (or fewer). Have the teams stand behind the starting line. The first players on each team rub the balloon against their hair until their hair has enough static to hold the balloon on top of their heads. Those two people then carefully walk across the room to the second marked line, balancing the balloons on the tops of their heads, then return the same way to their teams. The balloons are then handed off to the next players in line, who repeat the process (creating static, balancing the balloons on their heads, and walking the relay leg). If a balloon falls off, the player should stop in place and reenergize the balloon/head connection and continue on. The first team to finish wins.

NOTE If any children happen to be bald, they could be in charge of starting the race or judging the results.

GOING DEEPER

- In this game, we wanted the balloons to stick with us. What do you want to stick to you or with you in life (character traits, friends, adult role models, hobbies)?
- We created static to help keep the balloons attached. What is it that connects you with the things you want to hold on to in life?
- Static is energy. What gives you energy and makes you excited? What do you love to do? What are you passionate about or care deeply about?
- There was energy between you and the balloon. What is the energy that a group can give you?
- Do we feed one another (inspire one another) in positive ways?
- How can we continue to build and feed one another's positive energy?

ASSET CATEGORIES: Support, Boundaries and Expectations, Constructive Use of Time, Commitment to Learning, Positive Values, Positive Identity

Seven Up

5–10 minutes

SUPPLIES

- Seats (optional)

THE GAME Recruit seven game leaders to stand in front of the group. Tell everyone else to put their "heads down." All players should cover their eyes with their arm as they put their heads down (on their laps or their desks). After all heads are down, the game leaders wander through the group with each one choosing a player to gently touch on the shoulder. Once a player has been tapped, he or she should raise her hand. After all the game leaders have made their choices, they should gather back at the front of the group. Once all the game leaders are gathered, tell the players "Seven up!" Ask the players who had their shoulders tapped to stand. Taking turns, give each player a chance to guess which game leader tapped her or his shoulder. If the player is correct, then that game leader sits down and the tapped player becomes one of the game leaders. If the player is incorrect, then that game leader remains for the next round of play. Continue the game for as long as it is fun.

NOTE If you have a small group, you can adapt this game by choosing only three or four people to be the game leaders.

GOING DEEPER

- What clues help you determine which game leader did the tapping? What, if anything, gives the leaders away?

- Sometimes body language says a lot about what we are thinking or feeling. Why is it important to be able to recognize our own feelings?

- In this game you are chosen without always knowing who chose you or why. Has anyone ever chosen you to lead or do something and you didn't know why you were chosen? Talk about that time.

- Sometimes people choose us because they see a talent or skill in us that we may not even know we do well. Has anyone ever pointed out a skill or talent you have? What did that person point out?

- What is something you think you are really good at doing?
- What is something you really enjoy doing? Why?

ASSET CATEGORIES: Support, Empowerment, Positive Values, Social Competencies, Positive Identity

Four Square

TIME
5–15 minutes

SUPPLIES
- Sidewalk chalk (or masking tape)
- A large rubber ball

PREP Use sidewalk chalk or masking tape to create one large square on the ground; then draw a large + (plus) sign in the middle of the square to create four small squares within the large square. Number each square in one of its corners: 1, 2, 3, 4.

THE GAME Have one player stand in each of the four squares. The other players should line up around the Four Square board. The player in square 1 serves the ball by bouncing it in her square once, then gently hitting it into one of the other squares. The receiving player lets the ball bounce once, then hits it into another player's square. Receiving players are not allowed to catch or hold the ball. Play continues in this format. A player is out when:

- She allows the ball to bounce once in her square and then out of bounds (outside the square);
- She hits the ball *before* it bounces once in her square;
- She is hit by the ball;
- She does not hit the ball before its second bounce; or
- She hits the ball out of bounds.

Once a player is out, the other players move up a space (from 4 to 3, 3 to 2, 2 to 1) while the player who is out goes to the end of the line and a new player moves into the fourth square to play. Keep playing until everyone has an opportunity to play, or until enthusiasm wanes.

NOTE This game works best with 10 or fewer players, so if you have a larger group simply draw an extra Four Square board for each additional team.

GOING DEEPER

- What was your strategy to succeed in this game?
- How difficult is it to keep the ball in bounds?
- What are some of the things you have to do to keep your behavior "in bounds" at home? At school? Elsewhere in public?
- What are some "in bounds" rules we should set for how we treat each other as a group?
- What are some things that we should consider "out of bounds" for us as a group? What rules would those include?
- In the game, you got to move toward the number one position if you stayed in bounds. How do you think keeping your attitude and behaviors "in bounds" relates to moving up in real life?

ASSET CATEGORIES: Support, Empowerment, Boundaries and Expectations, Positive Identity

The Mannequin

TIME
5–15 minutes

THE GAME Select a volunteer to be the new Mannequin for a department store. Ask the Mannequin to leave the room. Once he's stepped out, ask the other players to choose a position they want the Mannequin to adopt for posing in the department store window. If the other players have trouble determining a position, prompt them with ideas. For example, the Mannequin could stand with his hands on his hips, lean against a wall, or sit with his hands cupping his face and his elbows touching his knees. Tell the group that when the Mannequin returns, you will tell him to strike a pose for the window. The other players should clap and/or cheer when the Mannequin gets close to the pose they have selected. If the pose isn't close to what they decided, then they should quiet down. Think about the game where you get hotter or colder. They should get louder as the Mannequin gets close to what they want, quieter if he's moving away from the pose they want him to strike. Once the Mannequin strikes the right pose, everyone should cheer wildly. Ask the group for any questions regarding their roles.

When you are finished answering questions, have the Mannequin come back into the room to begin play. Instruct the Mannequin to strike a pose for the department store window. His goal is to find the pose that the window shoppers will like best. He can move his arms and legs into various positions to determine the best pose.

Play as often as desired.

GOING DEEPER

Ask the Mannequin:

- What did you think when the crowd cheered or got quiet? How did that help you know what to do?

Ask all players:

- What does it feel like in real life when you know you have someone cheering you on and rooting for you?

- What about when a crowd of people boos you (says mean things, teases, bullies) or doesn't respond at all to what you do? How do you feel then?

- What can you do to not let others get you down when that happens? What can you do to respond positively in those situations?

- What are the signs and signals to you that you are doing a good job at school or at home? What signs do you like to receive to let you know that you've done a good job at something?

- Are there places where you need to make a few adjustments in order to accomplish what you hope to achieve? What are they? What can you do?

ASSET CATEGORIES: Support, Boundaries and Expectations, Social Competencies, Positive Identity

X-ray Vision

TIME
10–15 minutes

SUPPLIES

- Paper and pencil for each player
- One each of these creative containers: brown paper sack, cloth, a thin sock, a pair of thick socks doubled together (you could even use the fuzzy kind of socks), a clear plastic bag
- One each of these writing utensils: a ballpoint pen that works, a ballpoint pen that doesn't work, a mechanical pencil, a fine-point Sharpie, and a small paintbrush

PREP Put the pen that doesn't work in the plastic bag. Put each of the other writing utensils inside one of the remaining containers, without the players seeing you.

THE GAME Have players number their papers 1–5. Tell them that you want them to use their "X-ray vision" to guess what is in each container without looking inside and to record their guess about each object on their paper. Go around the circle, letting each player touch the outside of each container without looking inside or speaking. Each player then jots down her or his guess. After passing around all the objects, allow players to share their guesses out loud one object at a time. After each person has guessed, reveal the item to the group. Continue until the group has seen all of the items.

GOING DEEPER

- How much information can we gather through just one of our five senses? Just hearing, just seeing, just smelling, just touching, or just tasting? Aren't you glad that we are usually able to use multiple senses at a time?

- In this game, there were barriers that kept you from seeing the objects. Were some of the barriers more challenging than others for discovering the truth of what was really inside?

- What do the all objects have in common? What makes them unique?

- If we spent a little more time investigating the individual objects, and used more of our senses, what else do you think we would discover about each one and how it might be unique?

Demonstrate that one of the two pens doesn't work.

- None of us could have guessed that this pen doesn't work by touch or sight alone. We needed more information and we needed to spend time interacting with it to discover that it didn't work. How does that principle of spending time gathering information hold true for discovering the unique qualities of each individual person in this group?

- What are some of the things our group members have in common?

- What are some of the things that make each of us unique?

- What are some of the barriers that get in the way of our getting to know each other?

- How can we work around different barriers of language, religious background, or culture to discover how cool each of us is on the inside?

- What skills and attitudes do you need in order to appreciates others and make friends?

ASSET CATEGORIES: Commitment to Learning, Social Competencies, Positive Values

Little Professors, Little Einsteins

TIME
15–20 minutes

SUPPLIES
- Chart paper or a chalkboard

PREP On the chart paper or chalkboard, write a list of four categories, for example *games*, *sports*, *kitchen*, *school*.

THE GAME Divide the group into pairs. Show the list of categories to the players, and ask pairs to think of one thing they could teach from one of the categories to their partner. For example, the sports category might inspire someone to demonstrate how to do a corner kick; the kitchen category might inspire someone to show how to make macaroni and cheese; the games category might inspire someone to share a favorite game he or she made up to play with siblings. Give pairs at least 10 minutes to teach or tell each other about something they know well. Let players know you'll be asking for volunteers to share with the group. Allow additional time if players need it. Let as many groups volunteer to demonstrate or describe their new knowledge as time allows. Encourage shy participants, and tell all players to be proud of what they know.

GOING DEEPER

- What did you learn about your own abilities? What did you learn from other players?

- How did listening play a part in this game?

- Why is it important for us to listen to the expertise of other people?

- Why is it important to share what we know with others?

- What is something you are an "expert" in—something that you know a lot about?

- What is something you want to learn how to do well?

Celebrate the variety of things participants shared and learned from each other, and point out how everyone had something to share.

ASSET CATEGORIES: Empowerment, Constructive Use of Time, Commitment to Learning, Social Competencies

A Few of My Favorite Things

TIME

15 minutes

SUPPLIES

- Copies of the game card (one copy per team of three or four)

PREP Visit ❍ www.search-institute.org/great-group-games-for-kids to download a printable game card.

THE GAME Divide into teams of three or four, preferably with players who don't know one another well. Give each team a game card and instruct players to put a mark beside everyone's favorite item in each of the 10 rows. After five minutes, tell the groups to tally each row on their game cards, counting how many favorites the players shared and didn't share. For example, did everyone share the same favorite color, or did everyone have a different color, or were responses scattered across several possibilities?

NOTE This can also be a great intergenerational game to play because children can discover common ground with caring adults.

GOING DEEPER

- Which did you have more of: things in common or differences in terms of what you like?
- What did you discover in your conversations about your favorite things?
- Do you think any of your favorites will change as you get older?
- How does having things in common affect your friendships? How do differences affect your friendships?
- Do you think having a healthy balance of similar likes and liking different things makes a good friendship? Why or why not?
- What is one tip you would give others who struggle with liking people who are really different from them?

ASSET CATEGORIES: Support, Boundaries and Expectations, Social Competencies

Etiquette Relay

TIME
10 minutes

SUPPLIES

- Masking tape
- One each of the following per team of six to eight players: book, tennis ball, plastic teacup

PREP Use masking tape to mark two lines about 20 feet apart.

THE GAME Divide the group into teams of six to eight. Have teams line up at one end of the playing area. Each team is to walk to the other end of the area, turn around, and walk back, one player at a time. The catch? While the players are walking back, they must balance a book on their heads, hold a tennis ball between their knees, and carry a teacup with their pinky fingers extended. A player who drops a book or ball should start over again. If the player can't succeed after three attempts, another player can tag in to demonstrate this style of etiquette.

GOING DEEPER

- This game was about etiquette—having good posture, behaving well, showing proper respect and good manners. Why are manners important?

- What does having good manners say about you as a person?

- Every family has etiquette rules. Some families limit how much TV they watch while others may have the TV on all the time. When you visit a friend's house, what are some of the rules that family has that are different from yours?

- How can you show respect for the different rules other families have while still following the rules of your family?

- Different cultures also have their own etiquette rules. For example, in some societies most women wear dresses all the time, while in other cultures many women wear pants or jeans. Do you know of any different cultural rules that you're curious about? What are they?

If children in the room can speak to the differences, encourage dialogue. If the group is primarily monocultural, then explore the differences noted through research or having someone come in to speak.

- What is a nice way to ask others about their rules and etiquette?
- How can you show respect for and interest in learning more about them even if their way of doing things is so very different from yours?

ASSET CATEGORIES: Support, Boundaries and Expectations, Positive Values, Social Competencies, Positive Identity

Cultural Investigators

This game is recommended for grades 2 and up.

TIME
20–25 minutes

SUPPLIES

- One copy of the Cultural Investigators Worksheet for each group
- Large world map
- Computer with Internet access for each group
- Sticky notes, such as Post-it notes
- Pencil for each group

PREP Visit ❍ www.search-institute.org/great-group-games-for-kids to download a Cultural Investigators Worksheet or create your own. Compile a list of suitable Web sites to help players research the topic areas on the worksheet. You might consider weather.com, worldatlas.com, or national-geographic.com. Additionally, you might allow players to "Google" phrases such as "convention center, [their city]" or "sports team, [their city]." Be sure to double-check Internet sites to make certain they are safe. If possible, recruit a teen or adult volunteer to supervise the small groups.

THE GAME Spread out the world map on a table. Give each person a small sticky note to write her or his initials on. Have players close their eyes and place their sticky notes somewhere on the map. Group kids together according to how close their sticky notes are to each other. Ask players to share what they know about the area, and then go on a virtual scavenger hunt to find out more about the area. Give the groups 10 minutes to be private investigators and see what information they can find out about their areas. To add an optional element of competition, the game can be played like a scavenger hunt, with the winning team being the group that finds the most information in the allotted time. Let the groups share two or three cool things they learned about their areas.

NOTE If you do not have computer access, you could give young people a stack of related resource books and maps.

GOING DEEPER

- How did you find the answers to your questions?

- Each team shared information about places, people, and traditions. Which place would you most like to visit or learn more about? Why?

- What did you learn how to do in this game? What tricks to researching did you learn from your teammate(s)?

- What is something you are curious about? Where might you go to find the answer to your question?

- Why is learning how to find the information you want to know such an important skill? How can those skills help you at school? At home?

- What skills do you think would help you interact with others from a different culture?

- If you were building a Web page that others could visit to see interesting things about our culture, what would you include? (Go back through the map card and have players respond to some or all categories.)

ASSET CATEGORIES: Empowerment, Commitment to Learning, Social Competencies

Colorful Scavenger Hunt

TIME
15–20 minutes (can be adapted to take less time)

SUPPLIES

- Dry erase board, flip chart, or chalkboard and a writing utensil
- Paper and pencil for the teams

THE GAME Have players help create a list of all the colors they can think of and write them on the board or flip chart. Divide the group into teams of two to four, and have each team copy the list of colors. Give the teams 10 minutes (or less) to find items to match each color on their lists and write the names of the items next to those colors.

NOTE To adapt the game to be playable in a more limited amount of time, instead of generating a list of colors, simply confine the search for colors to what the players have within their team (clothes, backpacks, books, glasses, hair bows, watches, etc.).

GOING DEEPER

- What strategy did you use to find items?
- Did everyone stay together or did you separate to go get items?
- How well did you work together?
- What new things did you notice about your surroundings?
- What would life be like if we had only one color for everything?
- In life, not everyone is the same. We like different things, look different, are different sizes—and that makes life interesting. No one person is better than another. We're all special. How are you unique? How are others in your group unique?

ASSET CATEGORIES: Support, Constructive Use of Time, Social Competencies, Positive Identity

Team Play

> *Play gives children a chance to practice what they*
> *are learning. . . . They have to play with what they*
> *know to be true in order to find out more, and then*
> *they can use what they learn in new forms of play.*
> —**FRED ROGERS,** *Mister Rogers' Neighborhood*

Up to this point, the basics have been covered. Children know each other and are comfortably safe and relaxed. Now is the time for team play, because it is through team play that children practice everything they've learned so far and move things to the next level of play development. Team play is the prerequisite to developing higher-level team building, in which groups focus on building a team identity, fostering cohesion, overcoming challenges, and using critical thinking skills.

Team play helps children learn how *to begin* to work together as a group. In team play, children get to have fun and continue to build relationships, but they also practice cooperating and learning to work together. They get to do something they like to do and begin to see how others can enrich play and make it more meaningful by what they bring to the game.

Team play offers opportunities for children to take those baby steps toward building interactive skills (as well as motor and cognitive skills), learning to trust and rely on each other, and see each other as rich resources—friends who can have a good time together and help each other. The games in this chapter are geared toward providing space for those things to happen.

CREATIVE GAMES

Bring on the Band

TIME
20–30 minutes

SUPPLIES

- A variety of items that make noise when shaken (such as dried beans, pebbles, sand, dried noodles, keys, jacks, paper clips)
- A variety of containers such as canisters or boxes, or toilet paper tubes, paper plates, or other paper products (at least one per person)
- Supplies for each team: glue, scissors, tape

THE GAME Divide into teams of three to four players. Give players 5–10 minutes to make an instrument of their choice from the supplies provided. Have each team join with another group to form a band of six to eight musicians. Give them time to create their own signature song. After five minutes of rehearsal time, have each group perform. Consider awards for instruments: the most creative, loudest, most melodious, and so forth. You can also give awards for best team effort, best musical score, most likely to be used in a movie (you can even determine genres—action, comedy, science fiction, etc.), most likely to be sung, most likely to be picked by a rock star, and so on.

As a variation of this game, after the teams have created their instruments, you could elect a conductor to lead the big group in music of her or his choice (it can be a real song or something made up). Rotate conductors.

NOTE If there is a time crunch, have the groups create their instruments one day, then rehearse and perform at another time.

GOING DEEPER

- How did it feel to have the support of your small group when you were creating your instruments?

- What was it like to be part of a band and create music?
- How did you draw on the strengths and ideas of everyone in the band?
- In this game, you started with random everyday objects that you were able to transform into a musical masterpiece. How did that happen? What steps went into making your masterpiece happen?
- What can you learn from this activity about goals, planning, and decision making that can help you in everyday life?
- This game required creativity. How can creativity affect the rest of your life? Where in your life are you really creative?

Challenge your group to think about activities such as playtime, free time, school projects, art, decorating their rooms, and reading. For example, how could group members create another game out of recycled materials? How can they stimulate their own creativity and imagination to engage with the world around them?

ASSET CATEGORIES: Support, Empowerment, Constructive Use of Time, Social Competencies, Positive Identity

Magazine Drama

TIME
15–20 minutes

SUPPLIES

- Precut pictures from magazines, enough for two to four pictures per team of three players
- Paper and pencils for each team

PREP Clip pictures from magazines.

THE GAME Give two to four magazine pictures each to teams of three players, and let them create a script for a movie or skit to perform based on their pictures. Allow 10 minutes of creative development time. When time is up, have groups perform their skits.

GOING DEEPER

- How did everyone help? What job did each person have? What was your favorite job?

- How did your movie script evolve from the random pictures you were given?

- What skills did it take to create your movie?

- What role did creativity and imagination play in the process?

- Learning to create something (a movie) from limited resources (random pictures) is an important life skill. Share an example of how you have used limited resources to create something really cool. (If the groups need help, you could prompt them with a more specific question, such as "What if you found a really big box? What could you do with it?")

- If you could show others a "clip" from your life, what would you want to show them?

ASSET CATEGORIES: Support, Empowerment, Constructive Use of Time, Social Competencies, Positive Identity

Rhyming Words

This game is recommended for grades 2 and up.

TIME
5–15 minutes

SUPPLIES

- Paper and pens

THE GAME Organize players into teams of three or four and hand each team a pen and paper. Explain that you will say a word and, in two minutes, each team should list as many words as it can think of that rhyme with the given word. For example, if you say "dot," someone might write down *rot*, *hot*, *not*, *lot*, *robot*, and so on. After two minutes, designate one team to read its entire list aloud, one word at a time. If any of the other teams have written down the word that is being called out, then all teams should draw a line through that word. Rotate teams, having each read its list of words not already called out. Give one point for each rhyming word not named by another team and see which team wins. Note at the end any original words that weren't repeated by others. Repeat play with a new word *or* take all the original words and create an original song, story, or poem.

GOING DEEPER

- Do you think you would have come up with more words by yourself, or was this a better game to do as a group?

- There's a phrase that says, "Many hands make light work." What do you think that means? How do you think it relates to working together as a team?

- You had a starter word and then someone else came up with a new word, then another word, and so on. Did the new ideas come quickly and easily?

- Was there a time when the ideas slowed down? If that happened, did someone come up with a new word and then a whole new bunch of words were shared again?

- Sometimes working together comes easily and it's so much fun. Are there times when you've worked with others that it's been hard? What helped get you going again?

- How does this game represent the power of working together? Of being creative?

ASSET CATEGORIES: Empowerment, Constructive Use of Time, Commitment to Learning, Social Competencies

Name That Song

TIME
10–15 minutes

SUPPLIES

- One pen and paper for each team of four to five

PREP On the paper, print out a song sheet, featuring lyrical excerpts of many well-known songs. The following is a sample song sheet with answers in parentheses (a free handout version without the answers can be downloaded from ➲ www.search-institute.org/great-group-games-for-kids):

How I wonder what you are ("Twinkle, Twinkle, Little Star")

I love you; you love me ("The Barney Song")

Down came the rain and washed the spider out ("Itsy Bitsy Spider")

Won't my mommy be so proud of me ("Baby Bumble Bee")

Do they wobble to and fro? ("Do Your Ears Hang Low?")

Momma called the doctor and the doctor said . . . ("Five Little Monkeys")

There was a farmer had a dog ("B-I-N-G-O")

The one with the waggly tail ("How Much Is That Doggie in the Window?")

Three, four, shut the door ("One, Two, Buckle My Shoe")

Its fleece was white as snow ("Mary Had a Little Lamb")

Life is but a dream ("Row, Row, Row Your Boat")

You make me happy when skies are gray ("You Are My Sunshine")

And called it macaroni ("Yankee Doodle")

Round and round, round and round ("The Wheels on the Bus")

With a knick-knack, patty-whack ("This Old Man")

THE GAME Break the group into teams of four or five players. Distribute a pen and a song sheet to each team. Tell the groups that they will have 10 minutes (less for older groups) to write down the song title that corresponds to the lyrics on their sheet. When they are finished, go over each line and ask for answers. Reveal the correct answer. Let teams keep track of how many they get right. The team with the most points at the end wins.

NOTE For younger children, you can read the excerpts to the teams, one by one, giving teams time to write down the song title or draw a picture that reminds them of the name of the song to match to the lyrics you are reading to them. If the group is too young for this option, then simply have them run to you when they think they know the answer, and the first group to share the correct answer wins the point.

GOING DEEPER

- Which song is your favorite?
- Is there a song on this list that you don't know? Which one?
- What do you enjoy about music?
- Is music important to you? Why or why not?
- Can music affect your mood? How?
- If you had a choice, which would you do: write songs, play songs, listen to songs, or sing songs?

ASSET CATEGORIES: Constructive Use of Time, Social Competencies, Positive Identity

Name That Show

TIME
15–20 minutes

SUPPLIES

- Index cards and pens (one for each player)

THE GAME Give each player an index card and have all players secretly write down a cartoon, TV show, or movie they like. Collect all the cards. Break the group into teams of four and have them sit together. Have each team draw one of the cards from the stack. If none of the group members are familiar with the show or movie on their card, allow them to pick again. Give each team five minutes to re-create a scene to represent their show (they could also mime it). When time is up, let teams perform before the others. After each performance, have the other teams guess which show they were doing. Keep the other cards to use at another time.

GOING DEEPER

- How did you decide on what scene you would act out?
- How did you decide who would do which part?
- What was it like working together?
- Which team's choice was the easiest to pick? The hardest? Why?
- Was there any part of the activity that you particularly liked a lot (the creating, the acting, the watching, the guessing)?
- Now that you know this about yourself, is there something you can do with your newly identified skills or interests? Give an example or ask your teammates for ideas.

ASSET CATEGORIES: Support, Empowerment, Constructive Use of Time, Social Competencies, Positive Identity

Celebrity Dress-up

TIME
10–20 minutes

SUPPLIES

- Random clothing items from a closet or a dress-up box in a play area

THE GAME Designate one person to be the judge and two people to be the celebrity look-alikes. The judge calls out a famous person (TV star, singer, dancer, or even a character from a book) that the two contestants are likely to know, such as Hannah Montana or Snow White or Robin Hood. If the players have any questions regarding the choice (for instance, they don't know the person), they can ask the judge before he or she leaves the room. Once the judge leaves, the two contestants have two minutes to dig through the clothes to try to create an image that makes them look like the famous person. When time is up, the judge returns and determines which player looks most like the celebrity. Play as often as desired.

NOTE Should the look-alike be a tie, the judge can ask the celebrity look-alikes to mimic their celebrity. They can perform, speak, sing, dance, or what-have-you for the judge to break the tie based on talents. This is a good game for a small group, or you could have the whole group judge the two contestants.

GOING DEEPER

- Who was your favorite celebrity to pretend to dress up like? What do you like about that person?
- Which look-alike do you think was done the best?
- Who is someone you want to be like for real? What is it about that person that you want to be like?
- If someone chose *you* as the celebrity, what is something about *you* that you think others would want to copy, to be like?
- What is something you really like about yourself?
- What is something you like or admire in your teammates?

ASSET CATEGORIES: Constructive Use of Time, Positive Values, Social Competencies, Positive Identity

TIME
5–15 minutes

SUPPLIES
- Paper
- Pencils or crayons

THE GAME Divide participants into small teams of four to six (or do this as an individual event for one on one). Give each team a letter or number (the letter B or the number 10, for example) as a base. Each team should write the letter or number down on a piece of paper and try to create as many pictures as it can using that letter or number as a starting point. What pictures do team members see when they look at their letter or number? Give teams two minutes to create as many pictures as they can. For example, the letter B turned sideways might become part of a pair of glasses or the eyes on an owl, or scales on a monster's back, or even the pant legs of a boy. Have the teams draw all the pictures they can imagine.

When time is up, have each team show one of its pictures. Continue taking turns until all the pictures have been shown or as long as the group's attention stays focused. Determine the Crowd Favorite, the Most Complex, the Smallest Picture, the Most Use of Color, and whatever categories you can come up with to acknowledge something from each team.

NOTE If you want to add a competitive element, set the rule that a team is out if it shows a picture that's already been shown or when it runs out of pictures. The last team with a picture to show wins (the team that did the most original pictures).

GOING DEEPER

- What was your favorite picture, yours or another's? What was it about that particular picture that you liked?

- This activity required a lot of creativity. Why is it important to practice being creative?

- Creativity is something that helps you as a child and as an adult. How does creativity make it more fun to be a kid? How do adults get to practice creativity?

- What is something creative that you enjoy doing with other people?

- How does it feel to have people say nice things about what they like about your work?

- Do we take time to say nice things about and to each other every day?

ASSET CATEGORIES: Support, Constructive Use of Time, Commitment to Learning, Social Competencies

Film Writers

This game is recommended for grades 2 and up.

TIME
20 minutes

SUPPLIES

- Index cards
- Pens

PREP Make index cards with a *made-up* movie title—such as *Home Sweet Home*, *Kid Superstars*, *Wanna Be Me*, *Best Friends Forever*, *Rainy Day Blues*, *Game Time*—on each one.

THE GAME Divide the group into teams of four to five players each. Give each team a movie title, and say that teams have 10 minutes to create an original screenplay for their movies. They should describe the setting of the movie, the main characters, the plot, and the lesson viewers can learn by watching the movie. Option 1: Let teams share their screenplays with the larger group. Option 2: Let each group act out a one-minute scene from its screenplay.

GOING DEEPER

- How easy was it to come up with a script idea for that particular subject?
- What was the main point you hoped to make in your movie?
- If people were watching your life as a movie, what do you hope they would remember about you?
- In this game you had to work together, write, draw, act, create, and make decisions. In what jobs do you think you could use some or all of those skills?
- Does realizing that these game skills translate into jobs help you appreciate learning more? Why or why not?
- How else can you further develop the skills you want or need for a job?

ASSET CATEGORIES: Support, Empowerment, Constructive Use of Time, Commitment to Learning, Positive Values, Positive Identity

Playdough Film Studio

TIME
15–30 minutes

SUPPLIES

- Playdough (one small tub per person)
- A piece of paper and pen for each team of four to six players

THE GAME Each person creates a sculpture of some kind out of playdough. The only limitation is that the sculpture must be transportable. Allot two to three minutes for players to create their sculptures. Once time is up, group players into film studio teams of four to six. Each player should show her or his playdough sculpture to the team, then the team should work together to write the storyline for a movie based on the playdough sculptures. Give them five to ten minutes to create. Once time is up, have each group share its movie concept and the playdough sculptures its members used (if desired, groups can set up the sculptures in the order that they're used).

GOING DEEPER

- What part of creating did you personally like best: making the sculpture, creating a story, or telling the story?
- Did you like working by yourself better, or working with others?
- In the game, you looked at all the sculptures as a way to inspire your idea for a movie. What are things that inspire you when you look around you every day? What do they inspire you to do?
- What are the places and the people that inspire you each day to create or build or dream or work hard or do your best? How do they inspire you?
- Are there artists, musicians, or writers you really enjoy? What do you enjoy about them? What about their work inspires you?
- How can you be an inspiration to others? What do you hope to inspire in people?

ASSET CATEGORIES: Support, Empowerment, Constructive Use of Time, Positive Values, Social Competencies, Positive Identity

Box Art

TIME
20–30 minutes

SUPPLIES
- Boxes, such as boxes for crackers, cereal, instant oatmeal, or cake mixes (approximately 6–10 boxes for each team of four to six)
- Paper
- Scissors
- Tape

THE GAME Divide the group into teams of four to six. Give each team a stack of boxes. Give teams 10 minutes to create something with their boxes. They might make a circus train, a city, a skyscraper, a robot. After 10 minutes, rotate the groups around to a piece of box art different from the one they first worked on. Now, challenge the teams to take five minutes to write a commercial about their new piece of art. When time is up, have the groups share their work.

GOING DEEPER
- When you were first given the box, did you think you would be able to create anything out of it?
- If you had been given paper plates, what could you have made? What about paper towel or toilet paper tubes?
- You were able to make beautiful things with very few materials. How does that make you feel?
- Being proud of oneself is a good thing. You can be proud when you do your very best. The fact that you were creative and made something from nothing is definitely something worth being proud of. What skills and abilities did you use to create your masterpieces?
- You don't need much to be creative, do you? If you were to write a recipe for having fun, what ingredients would you include?

ASSET CATEGORIES: Support, Empowerment, Constructive Use of Time, Social Competencies, Positive Identity

Topical Poets

This game is recommended for grades 3 and up.

TIME

10–15 minutes

SUPPLIES

- Paper, pencils

THE GAME Give each player paper and a pencil. Assign the group a theme such as *animals, holidays, playtime*, or *favorite things*. Instruct everyone to take one minute to write down a phrase related to the theme. For example, if the theme is playtime, a phrase might be "Swinging on the monkey bars" or "Running across the playground" or "Bouncing balls." Randomly divide the group into teams of three to five players. Give teams five minutes to create a poem based on team members' phrases to read together to the whole group. Teams can add words, but they must use each of the phrases written by their members. At the end of writing time, let each team read its poem aloud together for the other teams to hear.

Keep in mind that teams may have a variety of interpretations about how to write poems, from patterns of rhymes to strings of unconnected words or phrases. This diversity and creativity is to be encouraged.

GOING DEEPER

- Was the theme easy to work with?
- What is another theme you would have liked exploring?
- A theme could be described as a message that comes across clearly in a song, poem, or story. With that in mind, what is a message you want to communicate to others about who you are?
- What is a value that you hope is a common theme in your life?
- What are the themes we want other people to see when they look at our group? What do we want to communicate about who we are?

ASSET CATEGORIES: Support, Empowerment, Constructive Use of Time, Commitment to Learning, Positive Values, Social Competencies, Positive Identity

Song Rewrites

TIME
10–15 minutes

SUPPLIES

- Paper and pencils
- Index cards

PREP On the index cards, write lyrics from songs the children would know, for instance, "The Barney Song," "Happy Birthday to You," "Row, Row, Row Your Boat," or "The Wheels on the Bus." (It's okay if more than one team gets the same tune.)

THE GAME Give the group a theme such as *happiness, rainy days, family time*, or *best friends*. Give everyone one minute to write down a short phrase that comes to mind related to the theme. Divide players into teams of three to five. Distribute an index card with song lyrics to each team. Give each team five minutes to create a song. They must use all their phrases (or the concepts behind their phrases) and fit the phrases to the tune of the song you gave them. When time is up, take turns having groups perform their new songs.

Example: "Row, row, row your boat gently down the stream" might become "Grow, grow, grow your friends, with fun activities."

NOTE If your group enjoys this activity, you could even have participants create a dance to accompany their song.

GOING DEEPER

- What was the best part of creating your new song?
- What was the hardest part?
- What would have made the challenge easier?
- How did you feel about your final product?
- Was this challenge something you thought you could do right from the start? Why or why not?

- You wrote a song. You created music. What is something else you would like to try that you haven't done before?

Assuming it's a good thing they want to try, you could ask the following questions:

- What seems challenging about it?
- What seems exciting about it?
- What steps can you take to make your goal happen?

If it's not a good thing that they want to try, discuss and redirect energies toward positive things to try.

ASSET CATEGORIES: Support, Empowerment, Constructive Use of Time, Commitment to Learning, Social Competencies, Positive Identity

Thumbprint Art Circles

TIME
8–15 minutes

SUPPLIES

- Ink pads with washable ink
- Paper or index cards
- Markers

You will need access to a sink so that children can wash their hands.

THE GAME Give each of the players a card or sheet of paper and ask them to make a thumbprint in the middle of it using the ink pads. Challenge each person to create a character or object out of the thumbprint by using markers or additional thumbprints. For example, show a picture of a thumbprint with a smiley face drawn on it. When players are done, gather all the pieces together where everyone can see them. Start a story circle using the thumbprint art, and have players weave their individual pieces of art into one big story.

NOTE There are books and online resources with lots of thumbprint art ideas, including animals and shapes, as well as different color inks. Use those if desired to help inspire ideas for what children can do to make thumbprint art. Tiles and scrap wood pieces can also be used as interesting mediums for creating art to take home to mount for display.

GOING DEEPER

- What are some other things you would like to create from your thumbprint?

- You made one little mark and it led to something big and beautiful. You can live your life the very same way. You can leave a mark on others by what you do and how you act. What is one thing you can do to make someone's day better? To make the world a better place?

- How can your behavior at home, in school, or in the community show that you are leaving a good "mark" of character?

- What do we want our "mark" to be as a group? What difference can we make together?

- What do we want others to say about us as a group? What's the mark of character we want others to see when they watch us?

- What mark of art will you create this week?

ASSET CATEGORIES: Support, Empowerment, Constructive Use of Time, Positive Values, Social Competencies, Positive Identity

RELAYS AND RACES

Superhero Teams Relay Run

TIME

10 minutes

SUPPLIES

- Masking tape

PREP Create a starting line and a finish line with masking tape.

THE GAME Break players into teams of four players. Have teams line up behind one of the lines. Tell players that each of their teams is made up of superheroes—Flash, Spider-Man, Superman, and the Hulk—in that order (the order they're lined up in). Each team has exactly the same superheroes—some are here from parallel universes! You're trying to find the team of superheroes that belong to *this* universe. The only way to do that is to put all the superheroes to a test of strength, speed, and endurance.

1. On "Go," the first person in each line, Flash, must run as fast as he can to the other line and back to tag Spider-Man.

2. When the second person in each line (Spider-Man) is tagged, she must walk on all fours (i.e., "crawl" up the walls) to the other line and back as fast as possible to tag Superman.

3. Superman, the third person in line, then spreads his arms out to fly across and back to tag the fourth in line—the Hulk.

4. The Hulk should then jump the distance across and back.

Repeat instructions superhero by superhero—ask the first person in each line to raise his hand; ask who he is (Flash); then ask how he is going to race across and back. Repeat the process with each position in line to make sure players understand how they are going to do their leg of the race. Declare the winning team *this* universe's superheroes.

GOING DEEPER

- If you could be any superhero at all, who would you be? Why?
- What is something you have to be strong to do in everyday life?
- What is something you like to be fast at doing (homework, chores, running, etc.)?
- What is something in your life that takes endurance? (If you need to give a definition, you might say, "Endurance is the choice to stick to something over time—even if it's difficult.")
- How can you give superhero effort at school? At home?
- What does a superhero look like for you in your real life? This person might not have superpowers, but he or she might have characteristics that are super admirable. Who comes to mind?

ASSET CATEGORIES: Support, Empowerment, Social Competencies, Positive Identity

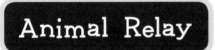

Animal Relay

TIME
10 minutes

SUPPLIES

- Masking tape

PREP Use masking tape to create two lines 20–25 feet apart.

THE GAME Group players into teams of five. Have teams line up behind one line. Give players one minute to decide which animal they want to be in this race: frog, butterfly, ant, snake, or dog. Each animal needs to be represented by one player from each team. Help teams decide if they're having a hard time resolving the issue.

Ask the frog from each team to stand behind the line. Once they are there, ask the players how frogs move. They jump! Each of them in turn will jump across the room to the other line and back to tag the next player in line. Tell them to remember what they're going to do. Have the butterfly players line up next behind their team frog members. What do butterflies do? Have all the butterflies practice flapping their "wings." Point out that butterflies seem to float in the air, so when it's their turn they should walk across the area flapping their arms as they go. Ask the ants to line up. How do ants move? They march! Have the ants take a few marching steps. On their turn all the ants will march across and back for their part of the relay. Have the dogs line up. How do dogs move? They run on all fours! Dogs on their turn will get on all fours and run across and back. Finally, have the snakes line up. How do snakes move? They slither! Snakes will get on their bellies and slither their way across and back.

After describing all the animals and lining up the teams, the game leader should start the race. When all five team members have completed the relay, they should sit down, signifying their completion of the task. Declare the winning team.

NOTE If teams are uneven, someone from the team with fewer people will need to be two different animals. This will make the teams even and the competition fair.

GOING DEEPER

- What other animals could we have used in this race? How would they have moved?

- If you could be any animal at all, what would you be? Why?

- The animals all move differently. Humans act and move differently, too. Do you think a frog and a butterfly could get along? What about a snake and a dog?

- What can we do to make sure we get along even if we are really different from each other?

- Why is it important to get along well with others?

- Without using any names, what's one step you will take today to get along with someone who is different from you?

ASSET CATEGORIES: Empowerment, Social Competencies, Positive Identity

Toss and Roll

TIME
10–15 minutes

SUPPLIES

- One Nerf ball (or similar) per team

THE GAME Divide the group into teams of 8–12. Determine a game leader for each team. Have teams line up in a straight line, shoulder to shoulder, facing their game leader. Game leaders should face their teams a short distance away (at least 10 steps). Each leader should have a Nerf ball. On "Go," each leader should toss the ball to the first person on his team, who then throws it back and sits down. The game leader continues throwing the ball back and forth to the other players until the last team member has thrown it back and sat down. Then the leader starts with the last person and rolls the ball to the seated player, who rolls it back and stands up. The leader works his way back until he reaches the end.

Need to add difficulty? Have a team start over if someone drops the ball.

GOING DEEPER

- What was the most challenging aspect of this game?
- What was it like to be the game leader?
- Was it hard or easy to keep the task in mind and do it correctly over and over (not roll when you should throw, etc.)?
- What was it like to be on the team when you weren't doing anything?
- Sometimes our role on a team requires patience and waiting while someone else is doing something important. When you weren't actively involved with the ball or the game leader, did you help your team in another way? How?
- In this game, you got one move down and then the move changed. How is that like learning? How is that like life?

ASSET CATEGORIES: Support, Empowerment, Commitment to Learning, Social Competencies

Kick the Can

TIME

20 minutes

SUPPLIES

- A can (or a ball)

THE GAME This game should be played in a large area with several possible hiding places. Select one person to be "it." "It" should close her eyes and count to 100 while the other players hide. When time is up, "it" searches for the players who are hiding. When "it" finds a player in hiding, that person will run back to "base" and try to kick the can before "it" touches the can. If "it" touches the can first, the other person becomes the new "it." Play until players get tired.

NOTE If a child is unable to count to 100, you could lower the number to 50 or the child could sing a short song.

GOING DEEPER

- Which part of the game was most fun to you? Was it the hiding, the seeking, or the racing and chasing?
- What is something you work hard to be first at?
- When you get beat by someone else, how do you respond?
- What if it's something you really want?
- Why is it important to both give our best and be happy with *our* best, regardless of how that compares to others?

ASSET CATEGORIES: Positive Values, Social Competencies, Positive Identity

Paper-Wad Fun

TIME
10–20 minutes

SUPPLIES

- Recycled paper (two sheets per player; be sure the paper does not contain confidential material)
- Timer
- Masking tape for marking lines
- Two garbage bags

PREP Use masking tape to make three parallel lines on the floor: two lines, one for each team, that are approximately 45–50 feet apart, and a dividing line down the middle.

THE GAME Divide the group into two teams. Have the teams line up across from each other just behind their lines.

Paper Pile: On "Go," have team members wad their pieces of paper as fast as they can and pile them in front of their lines. The team that finishes making all its wads first and sits down should yell "Stop!" when they are done. Award points for the first team finished.

Paper Launch: Line up the teams across from each other. They need to clean up and take out the trash. On "Go," each team should grab its paper wads and begin throwing them across the middle line onto the other team's side. Teams will have three minutes to throw as many wads as they can onto the other side and to keep their side as clear as they can. When time is called, every player should stop throwing. The paper wads will be counted on each side. The team that kept its side the cleanest wins.

Paper-Wad Relay: This time have the teams line up at one end of the room (both teams on the same end) and face the area where they just played Paper Launch. Have one player in each team hold a garbage bag. In relay style, have the first player from each team run to pick up as much trash as he or she can from anywhere in the playing area as you count to five out loud. Once five is called out, each player should race back, drop the trash in the bag, and tag the next person. Once the next player on either team starts to pick up trash, start the five count. The team that has the fullest bag once all the trash is picked up wins.

GOING DEEPER

- In the Paper Pile event you gathered as much as you could as quickly as you could. What is something you want to collect and gather for yourself?

- In the Paper-Wad Launch, you tried hard to get rid of your trash and push it off on someone else. If that were real life, would that be the right thing to do? What would you want to do instead?

- Sometimes we "hurl" insults or unkind words at others. What can we do instead to communicate when our feelings are hurt?

- Why is it important to help keep the Earth clean? What are some ways you can help keep this room or your neighborhood looking nice?

- Is it possible to be responsible and have fun at the same time? How?

- We made even the cleaning-up stage fun. What are ways you can make your chores at home fun?

ASSET CATEGORIES: Empowerment, Social Competencies, Positive Identity

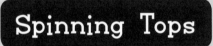

Spinning Tops

TIME
5–10 minutes

SUPPLIES

- One ball of yarn for each team of 10 people

THE GAME Players should line up in teams of approximately 10 people each. Give the first person in each line a ball of yarn. At your signal, the first player should become a spinning top, holding the end of the yarn strand in one hand and quickly wrapping the ball of yarn around his waist. He should then pass the ball of yarn to player number two (but continue holding the end of the yarn in his hand). Each player should become a spinning top, wrapping himself in the yarn, until the yarn reaches the last team member in the line. Then the spinning tops should all reverse to rewind the yarn back onto the original ball of yarn. The team to unwind and then rewind first wins the game.

NOTE For the more advanced spinning tops, have each player wind the yarn around herself two times each before passing the yarn on to the next player.

GOING DEEPER

- What was the most confusing or dizzying part of this game?
- When life gets a little confusing, who helps you sort things out?
- Is there something confusing right now in your life that you can name? What is it?
- When life seems too busy, how do you slow down the pace?
- Who supports you in the confusing or dizzying parts of life?

ASSET CATEGORIES: Support, Constructive Use of Time, Social Competencies, Positive Identity

Wacky Eating Relays

TIME
15–20 minutes

SUPPLIES

- One set of supplies for each team of 6–10 players: 2 small paper cups (such as Dixie cups), 1 plastic spoon, 1 piece of string (three feet in length), 1 doughnut, 3 pieces of bubble gum, 1 pair of chopsticks, 1 gummy worm, 1 small bowl, and 8–10 gummy bears
- A towel

You will need access to a sink so that children can wash their hands.

THE GAME This game should be played in a space that can get a little messy and potentially wet. Before you start the game, it's very important that all participants carefully wash their hands. To begin, divide the group

Balloon Gather

TIME
10–15 minutes

SUPPLIES

- Balloons (four to five per team of three)
- Masking tape (one roll per team of three)
- Blindfolds (one per team of three)

THE GAME Divide the group into teams of three players. Designate one player to be the balloon gatherer, one to be the balloon holder, and one to be the balloon spotter. Have each team blow up four or five balloons and place them at one end of the playing area. (It's okay if all the teams' balloons are mixed together.) Have the spotter and holder wrap masking tape sticky side out around the arms of the gatherer. Give them 45 seconds to wrap as much tape as they can around the gatherer's arms.

Once time is up, have each team blindfold its gatherer. Spotters should then go to the other end of the room. Their job is to help guide their gatherer toward the balloons without touching the player or the balloons. They should call out instructions to help guide the gatherers to pick up as many balloons as they can to carry back to the holders. Holders will take balloons off the gatherers and hold on to their catch. Gatherers can go back and forth as many times as they want within the given time limit. Give teams two to three minutes to collect as many balloons as they can. The team with the most unbroken balloons at the end of the allotted time wins.

NOTE For younger players, you might need helpers to tie balloons. Also, when gatherers are blindfolded, be sure to have an adequate number of people watching carefully to make sure they are safe from harm.

GOING DEEPER

- Let's talk about the game. What was it like to do your particular job? Spotters? Holders? Gatherers?
- How did you work together as a team? What were some things you did that went really well?

- What were some things that didn't go so well as you worked together? What would you do differently next time?

- The point of this game was to collect and keep as many balloons as you could with help from others. What is something you like learning and want to keep "collecting" more information about?

- What is a goal you want to accomplish in life? (For school? For overall health? For yourself? For home?)

- Who helps you work toward that goal?

- Who cheers you on?

ASSET CATEGORIES: Support, Empowerment, Boundaries and Expectations, Constructive Use of Time, Commitment to Learning, Positive Identity

Soccer Balloon Dribble Race

TIME
8–12 minutes

SUPPLIES

- Masking tape
- Balloons (two per team of four to six)

PREP Use masking tape to mark two lines at least 15 feet apart.

THE GAME Divide the group into teams of four to six. Have each team blow up two balloons—one is a spare in case the first balloon gets broken. Have teams line up behind a line and place their balloon soccer ball just in front of the line. On "Go," the first player in each line softly dribbles the balloon, soccer style, to the second line and back to the second player. Each player dribbles the balloon down and back one time. The first team to finish wins.

NOTE If there is an uneven number of players in a team, just let a player from the smaller team go twice in order to make the game fair.

GOING DEEPER

- Did anyone find a particular strategy to make this challenge easier? What was it?

- Did anyone share tips with the rest of her or his team for making things go smoother?

- How did you encourage and cheer each other on?

- This game required a certain amount of coordination. What are some other things you do that take coordination?

- Coordination takes practice. So does a sport, schoolwork, and reading. What are some things you practice? Can you see yourself making progress as you practice?

- What encourages you to keep practicing, even when you're ready to give up?

ASSET CATEGORIES: Empowerment, Constructive Use of Time, Social Competencies

Doggie Balloon Frolic

TIME
8–12 minutes

SUPPLIES

- Masking tape
- Balloons (one per team of four to six players)

PREP Use masking tape to mark the starting and finish lines.

THE GAME Form teams of four to six. Have each team blow up its balloon. Have teams line up behind the starting line and place their balloons just in front of the line. On "Go," the first player in each line should get on his hands and knees (assuming a doggie stance) and push his balloon with his head and shoulders to the finish line. Once the first player from each team crosses the finish line, he stands up and runs back to his team, bringing the balloon with him. Then, the second doggie player can start pushing the balloon. The teammates to finish first are declared top dogs.

NOTE This game can be played as an individual rather than team event if the group is small.

GOING DEEPER

- One thing dogs do well is play. Why is it important to play?
- Some dogs are not very nice. How do you keep safe when you are near people who are not very nice?
- Many dogs *are* social and friendly. Why is it important to be nice to others?
- How do you make others feel welcome?
- Dogs are often loving. Why is it important to show others you care about them?
- How do you show others you care about them?

ASSET CATEGORIES: Support, Empowerment, Constructive Use of Time, Social Competencies

Balloon Wheelbarrow

TIME
8–12 minutes

SUPPLIES

- Masking tape
- Balloons (one per team of three players)

PREP Use masking tape to mark the starting and finish lines.

THE GAME Divide the group into teams of three players. Have each team blow up its balloon. Have teams line up behind the starting line and place their balloons just in front of the line. Each team should determine who will be the wheelbarrow and who will be the two drivers. On "Go," the designated wheelbarrows will get on their hands and knees, and each driver will take a foot and hold it up so that the wheelbarrow is walking on his hands. The drivers will then push their wheelbarrows toward the finish line. The wheelbarrow will use his head and shoulders to push his balloon all the way to the finish line. If the wheelbarrow happens to fall during the race, or if the drivers lose their grip on his feet, they can simply pick up from there and keep going. The first team to finish wins.

GOING DEEPER

- What was the secret to accomplishing the task in this game?

- How did you communicate with each other so that the drivers were going at a speed the wheelbarrow could handle?

- In the game, the drivers guided the wheelbarrow toward the goal. Who is someone who gives you guidance toward goals you have?

- What "drives" you to do well in anything you take on? What makes you want to do well? This game wouldn't have worked for the drivers if there hadn't been a wheelbarrow. That was the tool they used to accomplish their task. What are some of the tools you have to help you do well in school? In after-school activities? At home? At your place of worship?

- What is a finish line you want to cross? What is the goal you hope to accomplish?

ASSET CATEGORIES: Support, Empowerment, Constructive Use of Time, Social Competencies, Positive Identity

Mr. Spider

TIME
10–15 minutes

THE GAME Mr. Spider sits with eyes closed, head down, in the middle of a circle in a large, open play area. The bugs (all the other players) make a circle around Mr. Spider. The bugs ask, "What time is it, Mr. Spider?" Mr. Spider says, "It's two o'clock," so players take two steps forward. If Mr. Spider says, "It's four o'clock," they take four steps forward. When Mr. Spider senses that the bugs are close, he says, "Dinnertime" and chases the bugs back to the edge of the circle. The bug he tags first becomes the next Mr. Spider. If he doesn't tag any bugs, he sits in the circle to try again.

GOING DEEPER

- What strategies worked well in this game?
- In this game, Mr. Spider talked about time. How do clocks and time help us at home, at school, and in other activities?
- What would happen if we didn't follow any sense of time?
- How can you be sure to respect other people's time (your teacher's, your parents', your coach's, your friends')?

ASSET CATEGORIES: Boundaries and Expectations, Constructive Use of Time, Social Competencies

Tennis Baseball

TIME

10–20 minutes

SUPPLIES

- Two to three tennis balls
- One to two tennis or racquetball racquets
- Bases to make a baseball diamond

THE GAME Add spice and even up the competitive edge in this variation on the game of baseball. Divide the group into two teams and follow the normal rules of baseball or softball except that pitchers will toss tennis balls and hitters will use racquets to hit the ball. The wider racquet provides greater odds that everyone will hit the ball.

For a variation on this game, use a Wiffle ball and bat instead of racquets and tennis balls.

GOING DEEPER

- Have you played baseball or softball before? How did you like this game compared to that experience?
- Are you more likely to try something if you think you might be successful at it?
- When you are successful at trying something, does that help give you courage to try something new?
- What is something you are nervous about doing?
- What is a step you could take toward doing that thing?
- What helps you take risks?

ASSET CATEGORIES: Constructive Use of Time, Social Competencies, Positive Identity

Crazy Ball

TIME
10–30 minutes

SUPPLIES

- A box of various objects that can be thrown or kicked (kickball, Frisbee, football, tennis ball, basketball, etc.)
- Bases to make a baseball diamond

THE GAME Divide the group into two teams. One team plays outfield and one plays infield. Place the box of objects next to home plate. The rules of baseball or softball apply in that there are three outs before teams switch places. In "Crazy Ball", there is no pitch, though someone can stay on the mound. The "batter" goes to the home plate and chooses three objects from the box. She quickly disperses them out onto the field (kicks a ball, tosses a football, throws a Frisbee), then runs the bases. The outfield players wait until the second object is thrown before moving to retrieve the items. Their goal is to collect all three items and return them to the box as quickly as they can. If the "batter" is between bases when this happens, she's out. If one of the objects is caught from the air, he's out. If she's safely on a base when the balls are returned, then she stays put until the next batter disperses three objects. The number of innings played is up to you (and the amount of time you have).

GOING DEEPER

- In this game, you had choices. What was your favorite crazy ball to use? Why do you like that ball in particular?
- When you have a choice to make about how you want to spend your free time, what do you usually want to do first? Why is that your first choice?
- What would happen if you always chose that activity to do in your free time? Would that be smart or not so smart? Why?
- You picked three different objects. Think about your friends. Are they all the same or are they different in exciting ways?

- What are some of the things you like about your friends? What makes them unique and different from each other?

- Can you think of someone who seems different from you that you'd like to get to know? How can you get to know that person?

ASSET CATEGORIES: Empowerment, Constructive Use of Time, Social Competencies, Positive Identity

Water Balloon Batting Practice

TIME
10–20 minutes

SUPPLIES

- Water balloons (five or more per player)
- Baseball bat
- Towels
- A flat object to represent home plate

PREP Fill water balloons with water and tie them. Give the players a heads-up to wear clothes that are okay to get wet, just in case. (You don't get very wet in this game.)

THE GAME Choose an outdoor area for the game, and divide the group into teams of three to six people. Teams should line up a safe distance away from home plate while the current batter assumes position over the base. The pitcher will pitch water balloons over home plate, and the batters, taking turns, attempt to make contact with the balloon. Batters get two points for bursting a balloon, one point for making contact with the balloon during the swing, and zero points for missing the balloon. As with baseball, batters are out if they miss contact with the balloon three times in a row, and the teams rotate positions after three outs, but there is no base running in this game. Teams should keep track of how many points they score. The team that accumulates the most points is the winner. Keep playing until all players have a chance to bat, or longer, if the group keeps enjoying the game.

- Did you cheer for your teammates, promoting a sense of support?
- Did you share your tips with one another, teaching each other the tricks of the trade (how you were able to be successful)?
- How did you treat the other team?
- Were you a good sport, whether you were losing or winning?
- Was this more about having fun and doing your best, or simply about winning?
- What is one thing you can learn from this game that will help you in other competitive events or sports?

ASSET CATEGORIES: Constructive Use of Time, Support, Boundaries and Expectations, Positive Values, Social Competencies

Follow the Leader Goes to the Playground

TIME
10–15 minutes

SUPPLIES

- Timer
- Paper and pen

THE GAME Take your group out to a playground area, and divide it into smaller teams of 5–6 or into larger teams of 10–15. Have each team designate a leader. Help the leaders determine an obstacle course for the teams to follow. For example, the course could go across the monkey bars, through a tunnel, down a slide, through the sandbox, across a seesaw, back and forth one time on a swing, and so forth. Designate one team to go first and have the other teams take a seat. On "Go," have the leader lead her or his team through the predetermined playground obstacle course. Time each team and record scores. The team with the fastest time wins.

NOTE If this game needs to be adapted for an indoor space, create an obstacle course using props such as cones, chairs, and Hula-Hoops.

GOING DEEPER

- What was it like to lead your team?
- What did you have to keep in mind to be a good leader (the path, keeping the team together, the goal)?
- Where did you have a hard time getting through the course? How did you overcome the challenge?
- Did your teammates help you when you were having a hard time? How?
- In this game you had a set course to go through. Life sometimes gives you lots of choices. How do you find the right course?
- What are some of the boundaries that your parents (or teachers or other caring adults) set to help you stay on the right course?

ASSET CATEGORIES: Support, Empowerment, Boundaries and Expectations, Constructive Use of Time, Social Competencies

Food Safety Note: If using food is an issue, use cotton balls instead. Make sure there aren't any food allergies in the group—some children have food allergies that are so severe they can't even touch certain foods without having a reaction.

Snow Fight

TIME
3–8 minutes

SUPPLIES
- Big marshmallows

THE GAME Break into teams and have an indoor "snowball" fight. Use this game to combat winter blues and to burn extra energy during trapped winter days.

GOING DEEPER
- What do you like best about snowball fights?
- What are some of the things you make with snow?
- What else can you do outside that you enjoy?
- What are some of the other things you like best about the winter season?
- What are some healthy ways to use all your energy when you're trapped inside because it's too cold to go out? What can you do that's fun and good for you?

ASSET CATEGORIES: Constructive Use of Time, Positive Identity

Marshmallow Monsters

TIME
10–20 minutes

SUPPLIES

- Paper bags containing a combination of colored marshmallows, toothpicks, and other goodies, such as Fruit Roll-Ups, licorice, or Froot Loops—one bag for each team of two players.
- Paper (optional)
- Crayons or pencils (optional)

THE GAME For Halloween or mad science fun, re-create Dr. Franken-stein's lab. Have partners create their own monsters from the bag of goodies you've provided. Give a time limit for players to assemble their masterpieces. Awards can be devised by the mad scientists and given to each monster (have the group designate its own award categories before viewing each monster—smallest monster, most likely to scare my sister or brother monster, scariest monster overall, and so on). Go around as a group to view the monsters, then vote on awards for each category.

OPTION The following is a way to extend the experience of the monsters from the lab and bring them to life. Plan for this additional activity to take 15–20 minutes

Continue the fun of making the monsters come to life by having the partners create a story and even draw pictures ("diagrams") of their par-ticular monster. Give them 8–10 minutes to create. Share stories with the whole group.

GOING DEEPER

- How did you and your partner work together to design your mon-ster? How did you share the work?
- Do you and your friends ever have different ideas on what or how to play? How do you resolve those differences?
- How can sharing make someone a better friend?

- How can thinking about another person's needs or wants make you a better friend?
- What can you do to be a better friend this week?

Marshmallow Sculptures

TIME
5–15 minutes

SUPPLIES
- Colored marshmallows, toothpicks, and other goodies (Fruit Roll-Ups, licorice, Froot Loops, etc.)

THE GAME Break the group into pairs. Give each pair supplies. Ask partners to create sculptures. Tell them a curator is coming to choose one of their sculptures to be a part of a traveling exhibit. Give them 10 minutes. Have the guest curator (another adult or young person) view all the exhibits and select a winning sculpture to go on display in the famous Hall of Marshmallow Art in New York, NY. For extra fun, take pictures of the curator with the winning creators and sculpture. Put the sculpture on display for a few days (unless it just has to be eaten!).

GOING DEEPER
- What do you like best about your sculpture?
- What do you like best about one of the other sculptures?
- Why is it important to think about what you like about your work (in the classroom, on the ball field, or playing a game)?
- Why is it important to take time to tell other people what you like about their work?

- Where did you get ideas for your sculpture? Who or what inspired you?

- Who inspires you to be and give your best each day?

ASSET CATEGORIES: Support, Empowerment, Constructive Use of Time, Social Competencies, Positive Identity

Marshmallow Olympics

Here are a series of Olympic events that utilize marshmallows. They might even inspire you to create your own Olympic activities! Note that the Asset Categories and the Going Deeper questions are found at the end of the whole Olympic sequence.

Marshmallow Shoot

TIME
5–10 minutes

SUPPLIES

- Masking tape (or cones)
- Wastebaskets
- Big marshmallows (or paper wads)

THE GAME Line players up (this can be an individual event or teams can send representatives) behind a starting line created with tape, cones, or some other object, and have them try to "shoot" their marshmallows into a trash can, tossing them overhand as a basketball player might shoot a basket. When players miss the trash can, they are out. Those players who are still "in" take one step back and shoot their marshmallows toward the wastebasket again. Players keep taking a step back after each successful hit until a winner is determined.

Marshmallow Toss and Catch

TIME

5–10 minutes

SUPPLIES

- Big marshmallows

THE GAME In pairs, each team tosses the marshmallow back and forth between themselves (playing "catch"). Whenever someone in a pair drops the marshmallow, both players are out. With each success, each team member takes one step back, increasing the distance between them. Continue play until a winning team is determined.

You could also adapt this game to be a timed event for getting the most successful distance during a set time. When drops occur, team members stand next to each other again and start over. When time is called, see which team has the most distance between them. (You could also designate someone as a counter for each pair and keep track of the most successful tosses for a given team. If this variation is used, have the teams start out near each other to get in some practice rounds, then have them take several steps away from each other until a challenging distance is created. From that point, have them try for the most successful tosses.)

Marshmallow Disc Throw

TIME

5 minutes

SUPPLIES

- Masking tape for a starting line
- One colored marshmallow per person

THE GAME This is a simple game of distance: how far can each person throw a marshmallow? Mark a starting line, give a three-count, and let them fly. The longest distance wins.

You could also choose to make it a "shot put throw" in order to vary how the players throw their marshmallows. Have them take the designated steps before throwing.

GOING DEEPER Process all the Olympic rounds in one debriefing.

- In which race do you think your team best worked together? What helped you work together well?

- What skills did you need for the different races? How were different team members able to "shine" with their skills during various races?

- Did you try something new that you liked? What was it? Why is it important to try new things, for instance, new foods, games, and sports?

- Who on your team cheered you on during the races?

- What's one way you can cheer on someone else today?

ASSET CATEGORIES: Empowerment, Social Competencies, Support

If you do the following games as a Water Olympics, the same teams can be kept for each activity. If water is too messy, you might consider using rice, shredded paper, or cotton balls.

Round One

TIME

5–8 minutes

SUPPLIES

- One cup of water per team of four to eight players (each cup needs to have an equal amount of water)

THE GAME Break the group into teams of four to eight, and ask teams to line up standing shoulder to shoulder. Give the first person in each line a cup of water. The cup holder passes the cup to the next person in line. Continue passing the cup down the line as fast as possible. The last person in line holds the cup for the judge to evaluate. The judge goes from team to team to look at how much water is in each cup. The team with the cup that has the most water in it wins.

Round Two

TIME 5–8 minutes

SUPPLIES

- One cup per person (one cup per team is filled with water)

THE GAME Have the teams of four to eight line up. If you played the first round of Cup Pass, the adjustment this time is to make sure that each player has her or his own cup. One person at the end of each line has a cup full of water. To pass the water down the line, it must be *poured* from cup to cup as quickly as possible with little to no spills. The team with the most water in its cup at the end of the line wins.

GOING DEEPER

- What did you do to prevent spilling water in Round One? In Round Two?

- If you weren't worried about spills, would this game have gone faster or slower?

- When is it important to do work slowly and carefully, instead of rushing through it?

- When might you need to do something as quickly as possible, even if you can't do it perfectly?

- There are times when it is important to work slowly and carefully, and times when you just need to do a task quickly. Which do you think you need to practice more of: doing work carefully or doing work quickly? How can you practice that skill this week?

- In this game you started with passing the cup, then added on the difficulty of pouring water. You did a basic step before adding in something harder. What is a real-life activity in which you practice a basic skill before learning something else harder (like dribbling a soccer ball before dribbling around cones)?

ASSET CATEGORIES: Empowerment, Boundaries and Expectations, Commitment to Learning, Social Competencies

Water Relay

Round One

TIME

5–10 minutes

SUPPLIES

- One bucket per team of six to eight participants
- One cup per team
- One jug of water per team
- Masking tape (or plastic cones for outdoor play)

PREP Mark a starting line and a finish line with the masking tape or plastic cones. Set buckets at the finish line.

THE GAME Have all teams line up behind the starting line and face the finish line, which should be some distance off and have a bucket at the end. Give the first players in each line a cup of water to put on their heads. They must cross the distance with the cup of water on their heads (they can use their hands) and dump the water in the bucket at the finish line. If the cup falls off, they must start over. Once they dump the water, they race back to tag the next person in line. Use jugs of water to refill the cups and the next person is off. Continue the relay until all team members have gone across. Determine which team has the highest level of water in its bucket, and announce that team as the winner.

NOTE See the Going Deeper questions at the end of Water Relay, Round Three.

Round Two

TIME
5–10 minutes

SUPPLIES

- Water balloons (one per team to start out, with extras on hand to replace balloons that break)

THE GAME Keeping the same teams, the goal is to cross the distance without breaking water balloons. The first person in each line crosses the distance with the water balloon between his thighs (probably a waddle), then carries the balloon back to give to the next person in line. Play continues. When (not *if*) water balloons break, have players start over with new water balloons. Keep track of the number of breaks for each team and deduct one point per break.

NOTE See the Going Deeper questions at the end of Water Relay, Round Three.

WATER BALLOON CLEANUP Give each child a bag and send everyone on a race to see who can collect the most balloon pieces. Whoever wins gets a prize, or give bubble gum to everyone who collects a good number of balloon pieces.

Round Three

This third round is recommended for grades 2 and up.

TIME
5–10 minutes

SUPPLIES

- One cup of water per team
- One bucket per team
- Multiple water balloons
- One jug of water per team

THE GAME For this third round, combine Rounds One and Two. Have players cross the distance with a water balloon between their thighs *and* carry a cup of water on their heads! At the end, they dump their water, then waddle back. You might want or need to shorten the distance for this challenging last round of water play.

GOING DEEPER Process all the water relay rounds in one debriefing.

- Which part was the hardest for you to do: balancing the cup on your head, walking while carrying the balloon between your legs, or managing both at the same time?

- What are some of the different things you need to balance?

- How do you manage your time in doing schoolwork, chores, and things you like to do for fun? What helps you manage it all?

- What is something you feel awkward doing (just like holding a balloon between your legs and walking)?

- Sometimes when we're learning new things it can feel awkward. What is something new you're learning or something new you'd like to learn how to do?

- What helps you keep trying and practicing until you can do something well?

ASSET CATEGORIES: Empowerment, Boundaries and Expectations, Social Competencies

Expressing Values through Play

Play can miniaturize a part of the complex world children experience, reduce it to understandable dimensions, manipulate it, and help them understand how it works.
—**JEROME SINGER,** professor emeritus, Yale University

Albert Einstein said that "play is the highest form of research." He's right; it's an opportunity to research more about how one thinks, responds, behaves, analyzes, and moves. One of the benefits of this highly interactive research can be discovered from *within* the heart and mind of those who are playing.

In play, there is an opportunity for all of us to explore values: What do we believe? What values do we hold? Why do we like those particular character traits? Why are they important to us? How do we maintain our values when we are faced with pressure to do something wrong? How do we stay true to ourselves when others would have us do otherwise?

Play provides the platform for children to search within themselves what they truly believe and why. This is indeed hard work! Through play, they have the opportunity to know themselves better, to discover what they're made of, and to decide who they want to be. Play can provide a fun way for children to begin to question, ponder, and explore the values they wish to hold. They get to stretch, bend, and mess with all the things they've been told to do and all the values that have been drilled into them thus far, so they can look at the whats and whys behind each value. In essence, children get to turn the spotlight on the various dos and don'ts of their lives, take them apart, inquisitively sift through them as they seek the answer to the question all children ask: "Why?"

There, in the midst of the "playwork," children begin to determine the values they want to keep as their very own. And then, they start to re-assemble their values, one by one, as they build their own moral compass.

The games in this chapter provide character-building moments in the Going Deeper sections and an opportunity for adults and children to ex-amine values together.

GAMES FOR EXPLORING VALUES

My Face Page

TIME
5–20 minutes

SUPPLIES
For the simple version:

- Paper and crayons/markers for each person
- Sticky notes

For the more elaborate version:

- Paper and magazines
- Glue
- Scissors
- Sticky notes

THE GAME Tell the group: "Today we get to be Web site designers. We will be designing our own home pages called 'My Face' pages that describe who each of us is. But instead of using a computer, we're going to create our pages on paper." Players should include words, pictures, or symbols to represent the following categories about themselves:

- A symbol to represent something they value
- Something they have done to help someone else
- One of their best character traits
- One thing they are proud they have done
- A goal they have for their lives (personal or career)
- Three traits they most value in a friend
- One thing they hope people say about them when they're not around to hear it
- Their name

Once everyone is done, post the pages around the room for others to see. Let players wander around to look at the pages and ask questions about what they see.

Make sticky notes available for players to use. Encourage them to leave notes on each other's My Face pages to encourage people or tell them of a trait they admire in them. Continue the activity as long as desired. This activity can be carried on throughout the day or even the week. Encourage participants to leave a note whenever they see someone doing something to help someone else out, or excelling in a difficult task, or exhibiting positive values in a tough situation. Challenge each person (youth and adult) to leave a positive note on everyone else's My Face page. This is a great way for caring adults to support children!

GOING DEEPER

- What was it like to create your very own page that was all about you?

- Was there a question you struggled to answer or define? What was it? Why was it challenging to answer?

- What is the most important thing about yourself that you want others to know?

- What is the thing you most want to know about someone else before you call her or him "friend"?

- On computers, we can create whatever image we want to portray. We can even pretend if we want to. In real life, we can't hide behind a pretend image. The image I have is really the person I am. It is "my face." Which image do you think is more important? Why?

- Why is it important to know the things you want to be known for and the things you want to work toward in life? What do you do to make those things come true?

ASSET CATEGORIES: Positive Values, Social Competencies, Positive Identity

Whose Story Is It?

TIME
10–20 minutes

SUPPLIES

- Paper and pens

THE GAME Give everyone paper and a pen. Invite players to jot down a true experience that happened to them that stands out in their memories: an embarrassing moment, something exciting or funny, an unexpected adventure, and so on. Give them five minutes to write. Remind them to put their names on their papers.

Collect papers and shuffle them. Randomly pull out three or four stories. Call out the names of the players on the papers. Have them sit in front of the rest of the players. Read each of the stories in random order. Challenge the group to determine which story goes with which person. Challenge the seated authors (the storytellers) to try to throw the group off by adding to the stories. They could try to claim any or all of the stories by adding facts to any given story as they try to convince the group that a particular story really is their story. After a little bit of storytelling, the group should vote. Reveal who goes with which story. Repeat as time permits or save the other stories for another time.

NOTE Pre-readers could play this game by drawing pictures rather than writing.

GOING DEEPER

- Storytelling is an art. Books tell stories. Art tells stories. Music can tell a story. What is your favorite way to learn or tell stories: books, art, music, or vocally?

- What is a skill you gain from telling stories to others? How can you use that skill?

- What was it like to guess the truth in this game, to figure out which story went with which person? What were the clues that helped you determine the right match?

- When is it important *not* to tell stories or to embellish? When is it important to tell the truth straight out? Why?

- How can we recognize the difference between telling stories for entertainment and stretching the truth?

- What is the story you want others to tell about you long after they've met you?

ASSET CATEGORIES: Commitment to Learning, Positive Values, Social Competencies, Positive Identity

My Experiences

TIME
10–20 minutes

SUPPLIES

- Index card and pen (one each per player)

THE GAME Distribute an index card and a pen to each player. Have players write down two things they have done and one thing they would like to do in their lifetimes. Challenge players to think of things that are unique to them that perhaps others haven't done and the one thing they most want to do in the world (a place to go, an event to participate in, a job to have, etc.). When everyone is finished, have players put their names on the bottom of their cards. Gather the cards, randomly choose a card, and read it out loud. Ask the group to guess who they think the card describes.

NOTE This activity works best for children who can write sentences, but you could adapt it by letting the children use simple phrases or draw pictures.

GOING DEEPER

- Did you write down any moments that you are particularly proud of? Which ones? Why?

- What did you hear from others' experiences that surprised you? Why were you surprised?

- Were there some similar stories or experiences?

- Were any similar dreams shared? What will it take to make those dreams come true?

- Can we help each other make dreams come true? If so, how?

- One way to work toward dreams is to set goals and write them down, noting the steps it will take to make them happen. Have any of you ever done that? Where are you in working toward your dream goal?

ASSET CATEGORIES: Support, Positive Identity, Social Competencies, Empowerment

Famous for Values

TIME
10–20 minutes

SUPPLIES

- Dry erase board (or chart paper)
- Dry erase marker (or markers)
- Scrap paper
- One pencil per team

THE GAME Divide the group into four teams. Give the teams a topic, such as *lying*, and ask them to think of a book or movie with a character who struggles with the given topic. When team members have an idea, they should write the book or movie title on their paper and stand up together but *not* share their choice aloud. One team player should take the paper to the dry erase board and indicate blank spaces on the board to correspond to the number of letters on their paper so that the other group can try to guess the book or movie. For example, if the topic were *stealing*, the player might think of the movie *Aladdin* and write _ _ _ _ _ _ _. They can tell the other teams whether it's a book or a movie. Then they slowly add random letters to the puzzle, until someone calls out the answer. Award one point to each team that guesses correctly. When the group's energy starts to wane, tally the scores and determine the winning group.

Sample topics:

Lying

Stealing

Bullying

Cheating

Irritating another person, just to be mean

Booing an opposing team

Physically hurting another person

Not being a good friend

NOTE If possible, leave all the completed word puzzles on the board so that you can refer to them during the Going Deeper reflection time.

GOING DEEPER

- Which topic was easiest to think of examples for?

- Which was the hardest topic to think of examples for?

- Talk about a few of the books and movies mentioned and what values dilemmas the characters had to solve. Did they make smart decisions?

- What would you have done in their situations?

- Sometimes it takes a lot of courage to do the right thing. What gives you the courage and strength to make smart choices?

ASSET CATEGORIES: Empowerment, Commitment to Learning, Positive Values, Social Competencies

PBJ Matches

TIME
15 minutes

THE GAME This game should be played in an open area and involve at least 12 players. Divide players into four equal groups. Tell the group that there are three parts that make up a great PBJ sandwich: peanut butter, jelly, and bread. Point to each group and assign it a label (there will be two groups that make up the bread). Tell everyone to remember her or his identity and find a place anywhere in the big group circle. Call out various combinations, and players should follow the directions. Go over each of the possible combinations of PB and J so that players know what actions to take with each of your calls.

Combinations:

- If the game leader calls out "Peanut butter toast" or "Jelly toast," then all the peanut butters and breads (or jellies and breads) must go to the middle and form toast pairs (e.g., one peanut butter and one bread) and lie down side by side on the floor.

- If the game leader calls out "Jar of jelly," "Jar of peanut butter," or "Just toast," then those players should hustle to the middle, join hands, and spin in a circle.

- If the game leader calls "Peanut butter and jelly sandwich," then four players (one peanut butter, one jelly, and two breads) should form a sandwich, with the two bread pieces holding hands around the peanut butter and jelly, and then yell out "PBJ!"

Players who don't find their match quickly or who complete the wrong action are "out" and join the game leader as judges on the sidelines. Keep quickening the pace and see which PBJ players are the quickest on their feet.

NOTE For an energizer, you can sing the song "Peanut, Peanut Butter . . . and Jelly."

GOING DEEPER

- How did this game get you to work with different people? How well did you work together with each pairing?

- Peanut butter is sticky. What do you want to stick to you? What values do you want to stick to your reputation? What do you want to be known for?

- When have you been stuck in a situation and didn't know what to do?

- Jelly is sweet. What adds sweetness and joy to your life?

- Bread can be plain and simple and nourishing. What are some simple things you enjoy just as they are (like a sunset or a cold glass of milk)?

- When do you like to keep things simple?

ASSET CATEGORIES: Support, Social Competencies, Positive Identity

Crisscross Circle

TIME
10–15 minutes

SUPPLIES
- One blindfold

THE GAME Gather the group in a big circle. Ask one person to volunteer as the Crisscross Catcher (the Triple C). Tell the other players to remember their numbers as you number them off starting with 1. After blindfolding the Triple C, ask him to call out two numbers between one and ___ (however many players are in the group). When he calls out the two numbers, the two corresponding players should walk (not run!) across the circle, trying to change places. Meanwhile, the Triple C will try to tag the two players as they crisscross. If he tags one of the players, that tagged player swaps places with him and becomes the new Triple C, while he assumes the number of the tagged player. If he doesn't tag anyone, he should call out two different numbers and try again. Continue play accordingly for about 10 minutes—keep an eye on players' energy levels. Since the Crisscross Catcher is blindfolded, several volunteers should watch out for his safety during this activity.

GOING DEEPER
- How did it feel to be part of the circle? Were you rooting for Triple C or the sneakers? How did you decide whom to root for?
- When you are trying to accomplish a difficult task, it sometimes feels like you are blindfolded, because you don't know how to do the work. What is a hard task you are trying to learn, and how can you get help to "remove" your blindfold and succeed at what you're trying to do?

- What is a character trait (such as honesty, responsibility, or fairness) that is difficult for you? What can help you get better at living out that particular trait?

- How did it feel to try to sneak across the circle without being tagged?

- When do people sometimes try to "sneak around" in daily life?

- Oftentimes when we feel the need to sneak, we've done something wrong. What commitments can we make today to ensure that we won't need to sneak around?

ASSET CATEGORIES: Support, Commitment to Learning, Positive Values, Social Competencies

Spinners

TIME
10–15 minutes

SUPPLIES

- A bag of simple scenarios (see Prep)

PREP Write various scenarios on cards and put them in a bag, or visit ❍ www.search-institute.org/great-group-games-for-kids to download a printable version of the Spinners Sample Scenarios and cut the questions into strips.

THE GAME The group should sit or stand in a circle around one volunteer, who is the Spinner. The Spinner closes her eyes and spins around in place, pointing to a random player in the outside circle. The person who is pointed to should draw a card from the bag and read the brief scenario to the group. The person on his left should give a quick example of a "wrong way" a young person could respond. The person on his right should give a quick example of a "right way" a young person could handle the situation. The Spinner should choose the best actor (the one who gave the most convincing performance) to be the next Spinner.

GOING DEEPER

- Which role was easier: coming up with a wrong solution or a right one? Why?

- What were some of the responses acted out that you want to remember when you are in a tricky situation?

- What helps you make the best decision when you are faced with a tough situation?

- Share a tough decision you made that you are proud of.

- Share a decision that you are not proud of, and share how you would respond now if you had a "do over."

- How can you encourage one another to make good choices when you are facing tough decisions?

ASSET CATEGORIES: Support, Boundaries and Expectations, Positive Values, Social Competencies

Goldilocks and the Three Bears

TIME
15 minutes

SUPPLIES

- Paper and a marker

PREP Make signs to label three corners: Little Bear, Mama Bear, Papa Bear. If you are playing this game with pre-readers, use picture signs of the three bears.

THE GAME Point out the three corners labeled Little Bear (representing a little), Mama Bear (representing medium), and Papa Bear (representing huge). Tell the players that they are all Goldilocks in this game and they should choose the bear of their choice for each question. Ask players values-based questions, and invite them to respond by walking to the corner of the room that best matches their opinion. Depending on the question, invite players to share their opinions out loud after they move to their bear corners.

Here are some practice questions:

- Goldilocks, how much do you like to run and play? A little bit (Little Bear), sometimes (Mama Bear), a whole lot (Papa Bear)?

- Goldilocks, how much do you like to eat fruits and veggies each day? A little bit (Little Bear), sometimes (Mama Bear), a whole lot (Papa Bear)?

- Goldilocks, how much do you value your parents' opinions? A little bit (Little Bear), a medium amount (Mama Bear), a whole lot (Papa Bear)?

- Goldilocks, how much do you value your friends' opinions? A little bit (Little Bear), a medium amount (Mama Bear), a whole lot (Papa Bear)?

- Goldilocks, how much do you think you should show respect to others through your language and behavior? A little bit (Little Bear), a medium amount (Mama Bear), a whole lot (Papa Bear)?

- Goldilocks, how often do you expect yourself to be nice and caring? A little bit (Little Bear), a medium amount (Mama Bear), a whole lot (Papa Bear)?

- Goldilocks, how much do you value helping others when you see they need help? A little bit (Little Bear), a medium amount (Mama Bear), a whole lot (Papa Bear)?

GOING DEEPER

- For which question did you think it would be easiest for you to do the right thing all the time?

- What is one value that you really struggle with?

- Who helps you to make smart decisions?

- How can you be sure to do the things you know to be right?

- If you aren't sure whether something is right or wrong, how do you find out?

- Can you think of a time when two values seem to bump heads and it seems like you have to choose between two good things? (For example, you get a homemade present from your aunt. You love that she made it, but you don't like what she made. That's an example of caring versus honesty if she asks you how you like it.) What can you do when values seem to conflict?

ASSET CATEGORIES: Support, Boundaries and Expectations, Positive Values, Positive Identity

Nursery Rhymes Quiz

TIME
10 minutes

SUPPLIES

- One printed Nursery Rhymes Quiz per player or per team of three or four

PREP A free handout version of the quiz can be downloaded from ➲ www.search-institute.org/great-group-games-for-kids. The answer key is as follows:

Which nursery rhyme is associated with each phrase?

Two small children tumbling down	"Jack and Jill"
An egg gets all cracked up	"Humpty Dumpty"
City landmark falling down	"London Bridge Is Falling Down"
A small animal and a loud pop	"Pop! Goes the Weasel"
Talking black farm animal	"Baa Baa Black Sheep"
Around and around the roses	"Ring around the Rosie"
Small insect crawling up a spout	"Itsy Bitsy Spider"
A clock chimes and furry animals climb	"Hickory Dickory Dock"
A light flashing in the night	"Twinkle, Twinkle, Little Star"
Three unseeing animals running	"Three Blind Mice"
Wishing on the night's first light	"Star Light, Star Bright"
Asking about neighbors at Drury Lane	"The Muffin Man"

THE GAME Give each player (or team) a copy of the nursery rhymes quiz. Allow three minutes for players to try to correctly identify the actual nursery rhymes based on the clues. When time is up, go over the answers and see how well the players did.

NOTE For pre-readers, you can ask the questions out loud to the whole group, or you can have an adult volunteer work with each group to write down the words for them.

GOING DEEPER

- Is there a lesson you can learn through the story of your favorite nursery rhyme? What is it?
- How are stories, poems, and rhymes great ways to share values and life lessons?
- Why are values important for us to talk about and follow?
- Do you think this game is easier to play by yourself or with others? Why?
- How can you continue to help one another on future tasks?

ASSET CATEGORIES: Support, Empowerment, Commitment to Learning, Positive Values

Ooey Shoey Sharing

TIME
15 minutes

THE GAME This group should have at least 10 players. To "kick off" the game, start by having everyone take off just one shoe and place it in a pile at the front of the room. Then everyone should hobble on one shoe to the back of the room. On the game leader's call, each person should hobble back to the shoe pile, pick up a random shoe, and hunt for the shoe's owner. In payment for the return of the shoe, the Shoe Owners should each share two values (such as honesty, trustworthiness, or love) that they think are really important, and the Shoe Givers should try to remember everything the Shoe

Owners say. Give everyone five minutes to return the shoes and get to know the shoes' owners, then regroup in a large circle to let the Shoe Givers introduce the Shoe Owners along with the new facts they learned about them.

GOING DEEPER

- How did you decide which values to pick out of all the options that are available? What makes the ones you selected so important to you?
- How well did you listen respectfully to your Shoe Owner?
- Did you ask your Shoe Owner any questions to learn more about what he or she was telling you?
- What did you learn about each other?
- Did we put caring and respect into play when we introduced each other to the rest of the group at the end?
- What is one thing we can do to show respect and caring the rest of the day?

Asset Categories: Support, Commitment to Learning, Positive Values, Social Competencies, Positive Identity

TIME
20 minutes

SUPPLIES

- Three balls (or something else to represent honey)

THE GAME This game should have a large playing area with hiding places (such as trees, playground equipment, tables). Divide the playing area in half by telling everyone the boundary markers. Split the group into two teams, the Bees and the Bears. With the Bears facing the opposite direction, the Bees should silently hide their honey (three balls) in one place within their playing area. On the game leader's count, the Bears will run from their half of the playing area into the Bees' playing area to find the beehive and take the honey back to their territory. A single Bear cannot carry more than one of the balls. The Bees swarm and try to tag the Bears. Bears who are tagged go back to their half of the playing field. Swap teams when all the honey has been taken or when the game leader calls time.

GOING DEEPER

- The Bears had to work together to get the Bees' honey. Think of a time when you need to work with others to achieve a goal. Share some examples.
- What are things a team can do to work well together?
- What are specific ways that *you* can contribute to the success of a team that you are on?
- The honey was made by the Bees. Sometimes bees get mad when others mess with what they've made. What is something you've made that you were proud of?
- How do you feel when others mess with something you've worked hard on?
- How can we show respect for one another's work and belongings?

ASSET CATEGORIES: Support, Empowerment, Constructive Use of Time, Positive Values, Positive Identity

Dumpty Humpty

This game is most appropriate for grades 3 through 5.

TIME
10–15 minutes

SUPPLIES

- Printed lyrics for four or five different nursery rhymes

PREP Cut the nursery rhymes into two-line stanzas so that you can give a copy of each section to a different team. Be careful to keep the different nursery rhymes clipped together, or you'll create a whole new game of nursery rhyme mix-ups!

THE GAME Divide into five or six groups (or however many nursery rhyme sections you have). Give each group its two-line stanza of the first nursery rhyme. Give the groups three minutes to rewrite its section of the nursery rhyme, trying to be creative and funny. Then let each group read its stanzas in order. Let each team vote for the group (other than themselves) that had the funniest rewrite. Award one point to the funniest team. Repeat the process with a few more nursery rhymes to determine the overall winner.

Example: Humpty Dumpty sat on a wall; Humpty Dumpty had a great fall.

Rewrite: Humpty Dumpty went to the mall; Humpty Dumpty bought a rag doll.

GOING DEEPER

- What were some of the funniest rhymes we wrote together?
- Do you think we were more creative in our small groups or as a big group when everything came together?
- Did you have ideas you thought of that you weren't willing to share out loud? What sometimes keeps you from sharing what you think?
- How can you continue to have the confidence to share your thoughts and ideas?
- Why is it important for us to do our part to help others feel safe to share their feelings, opinions, values, and ideas?
- What can we do to make this group a safe place to share what we believe and feel?

ASSET CATEGORIES: Support, Constructive Use of Time, Commitment to Learning, Positive Values, Social Competencies, Positive Identity

The Animal Game

TIME
10–15 minutes

THE GAME Each player chooses an animal and a movement to match the animal. For example, a player might choose to be a rabbit by bouncing in place with her legs together and using her hands to make long ears over her head. Everyone stands in a circle. For the first round, one after another around the circle, players show their own movement to the group. For the next round, you should pick one person to start. That person does his movement, then one other player's movement. The person whose movement was done then does her own movement and then a different person's movement. If a player takes too long to do someone else's movement or does the movement incorrectly, then that player is out and must exit the circle. The player is also out if he or she does the movement of someone who is already out. When it gets down to two players, declare both players the alphas of the animal kingdom. The whole game is played without saying anything (but you, as the game leader, can remind players that they're out, and players who are out can cheer for players who are still in the circle).

GOING DEEPER

- What strategies helped you be successful in this game?
- Can you use any of these strategies to help with other experiences in life, such as sports, school, homework, hobbies, or relationships?
- In this game, you taught others your own move and you learned theirs. In real life, what is something neat you've learned from someone else, or about someone?
- What is something you hope others learn from you?
- Think of a value or character trait that you want to be known for (your "signature move"). What is the value? Give an example of how others will see that value at work in your life.

ASSET CATEGORIES: Constructive Use of Time, Commitment to Learning, Positive Values, Social Competencies

Elements of Challenge

A child loves his play, not because it is easy, but because it is hard.
—**BENJAMIN SPOCK,** American pediatrician

It doesn't take much for play at any stage of the game to become competitive. That is a given. Some humans are more competitive than others and have to have the goal or the win to work toward. They bring that competitive edge with them. But, for this chapter, don't let the word *challenge* confuse you. It is not meant to be indicative of competition. Rather, it points more toward courage.

Every person, every group goes through growing pains. In fact, both individuals and groups can become stagnant or plateau in their development unless there are elements of challenge along the way to promote growth. Challenge is a natural part of life. It often shows up in our lives as changes, as transitions, as obstacles, or as simply "new"—new things to learn, new tasks, new activities, new people, new places.

Facing a challenge alone can be daunting for some, whether that challenge is physical, or whether it is vocal and calls for a voiced opinion or value. Facing a test as part of a group can be less lonesome, perhaps, but equally hard on our nerves and sense of self, especially when we are dealing with the unknown. It is that "unknown" that is the kicker.

The Roman poet Ovid said that "in our play, we reveal what kind of people we are." Challenge reveals character and what we're made of as well as where we need to grow. Learning how to handle challenges and to develop skill sets that enable us to face trials with confidence is an important part of being an individual and being in a group. Thus the earlier reference to courage—it takes courage to stand on one's own two feet, and it takes courage to embrace challenges. But the result is often confidence—confidence in one's own abilities and the belief that one can face the unknown and excel.

The games in this chapter address both sides of the equation. They include challenges for individual play where children have to decide what they will do and the completion of an activity lies solely on them. And it offers games to challenge groups to deal with obstacles together and figure out how they will work as a team to be successful.

Prince Charming Race

TIME
5–10 minutes

SUPPLIES

- Shoes
- Masking tape
- Timer

PREP Clear a playing area, marking it using masking tape for a starting/finish line.

THE GAME Have all the players take off their right shoes and pile them up in the middle of the playing area. Mix up the shoes. Tell the players that the missing pages from the fairy tale of Cinderella reveal that not only did Cinderella lose her shoe, but Prince Charming, in his determination to find her, took off his shoe and ran around in hers because he didn't want to lose her shoe. He needed it to find her. But now his feet really hurt; he's not moving very fast and he thinks it might be better if he looked for her in his own shoes and just carried hers. There's one problem: he can't find his own shoe! He needs to hurry, get his shoe, and run after Cinderella. Time is running out! It is 15 seconds before the clock strikes midnight. Have players line up at the starting line. On the count of three, start the 15-second countdown while players hobble (because his feet hurt, remember?) to the pile, find their shoes, put them on, and race back to the starting/finish line. See who makes it before midnight strikes. Play more rounds and set goals to improve times if desired.

GOING DEEPER

- What was your favorite part of the Cinderella story?
- If you could rewrite some part of the story, what would you change?

- Have you ever lost anything that was important to you? What was it?
- Did you find it or did it stay lost forever? How did you react?
- Did you feel stress racing against the clock in this game? What are other things that cause you to get upset or feel stress?
- What helps you deal with pressure positively?

ASSET CATEGORIES: Commitment to Learning, Social Competencies, Positive Identity

Matched Sets

TIME
5–10 minutes

SUPPLIES

- One pen and piece of paper per player

THE GAME Distribute the pens and paper. Ask players to number their paper from 1 to 10. Tell them that you are going to call out a name and everyone should write down a name to make it a complete matched set. For example, if you say "Hansel," they should write down "Gretel." When they are finished, review each paper and see who matched the most sets correctly.

Sample list to pull from:
Shrek—Fiona
C-3PO—R2-D2
Fred Flintstone—Wilma Flintstone or Barney Rubble
Batman—Robin
Shaggy—Scooby Doo
Snoopy—Woodstock or Charlie Brown
Superman/Clark Kent—Lois Lane
Cinderella—Prince Charming
Dora—Diego or Boots
Curious George—Man in the Yellow Hat

Buzz Lightyear—Woody

Winnie the Pooh—Piglet, Eeyore, or Christopher Robin

Ernie—Bert

Miss Piggy—Kermit

Be sure to update your list of chosen pairs regularly, in order to feature characters with whom the players will be most familiar.

NOTE Some sets may have more than one possible match. For younger children with limited reading skills, print a game card with one set of characters listed on the left side and the matching characters listed in random order on the right side. Let players draw a line to connect each matching set.

GOING DEEPER

- This game was about pairs that go together. What are other things that naturally go together?

- If someone asked you to match a value with your name, which would you choose as your natural match: caring, honest, respectful, nice, responsible, or trustworthy? Why do you think that particular value is your match?

- Is there another value you would like to be paired with your name? Which one? Why?

- Who is someone in your life that is part of your "matched set"? Who is someone you like to spend time with?

- What do you like to do with that person?

- How are you a good influence on that person? How is he or she a good influence on you?

ASSET CATEGORIES: Support, Positive Values, Social Competencies, Positive Identity

Run, Rabbit, Run

TIME
10–15 minutes

SUPPLIES

- Tape or chairs to mark the boundaries of the playing area

THE GAME Pick two players to be the Wolves. Have all the other players stand on the other end of the playing area. The Wolves will call out, "Run, Rabbit, run!" to start the game. When they make their call, all the other players should run for the line on the other side of the playing area and try to avoid being tagged by the Wolves. If they are tagged before reaching the far boundary, then they should freeze and sit down where they were tagged. Tagged players become part of the forest and are Trees. Their new role is to try to tag other running players from where they are sitting. They can use their arms but not their legs to tag others.

Once all players have been tagged or reached the safety of the boundary for the round, then the Wolves move to the other end of the playing area to start the next round. Play continues until only two Rabbits are left. The two remaining Rabbits are the winners. If time allows, have the winners become the new Wolves for another round of play.

GOING DEEPER

- Which part did you like better: being a Wolf, a Rabbit, or a Tree? Why?

- What strategy did you use to try to avoid the wolves? How well did it work?

- The Wolves were trying to catch you. Name some of the "bad wolves" you want to avoid in your everyday life. What are some of the things that try to catch you and get you into trouble? How can you avoid them?

- What can you do if you see someone being a "bad wolf" (bully) at school? How can you help?

- In this game, some of your own friends fell victim to the Wolves and they joined the Wolf team! They tried to keep you from reaching your goal. If you see a friend make a bad choice in real life, how can you help her or him?

- If a friend tries to stop you from doing something good or tries to keep you from being safe, what can you do?

ASSET CATEGORIES: Boundaries and Expectations, Constructive Use of Time, Social Competencies, Positive Identity

Trio Battles

TIME
15 minutes

THE GAME This game is a lot like Rock, Paper, Scissors, but it has much bigger motions. For every round, you will have three choices:

Gorilla: roar and beat your hands against your chest.

Human: stand tall with your hands on your hips.

Feather: wiggle your fingers and say, "Tickle, tickle."

Each choice has a strength and a weakness:

- The gorilla always beats the human because it is stronger.
- The human beats the feather because he plucked it.
- The feather beats the gorilla because it tickles the gorilla.

Have everyone find a partner and stand back to back. When the game leader says "Go," both partners must turn around immediately to reveal their mode of operation. If there is a tie, players should quickly replay to declare a winner. Whoever wins the round stays in the game and finds another partner. Players who are beaten make a circle around the other players to see who has the best luck. The last person standing wins the game.

GOING DEEPER

- Did you have good luck with any character in particular? Which one?
- What is the strength of that character? What is its weakness?
- How has physical strength helped you in life?

- How has brain power and being able to use your head helped you in different situations?

- Luck determined whether you and your challenger did the same motion—you had very little control over the outcome. What is a challenging situation you're facing in which you can control what happens?

- How can you be sure not to use laughter to hurt others, but always to help others?

- How can you be sure not to use your strength to hurt others, but to help instead?

ASSET CATEGORIES: Support, Boundaries and Expectations, Positive Values, Social Competencies, Positive Identity

Radio Songs

TIME
5–15 minutes

THE GAME Ask for a volunteer to start the game by singing a song out loud over and over. Another player may change the channel on the radio at any time by cutting in and singing a different song. The first player stops singing as soon as the new person begins her song. Each singer should be able to get at least two lines out before someone changes the radio and interrupts with a new song. A player is out if he repeats a song that's already been "played" or if no one interrupts and he can't continue the song he started singing. Play until it gets old (the radio loses its signal) or until you have a winning soloist.

If you want to add a dimension of difficulty, challenge the group to choose songs with themes or to show some sort of connection. For example, all songs must reflect a weather theme ("It's raining, it's pouring . . ." might be followed by "Oh, the weather outside is frightful, but the fire . . .").

GOING DEEPER

- How many different songs did you come up with?

- What is one of your favorite songs ever? Why?

- What would have made this challenge easier?
- When you have challenges that are hard, what do you do to overcome the hard part? How or where do you find help?
- What helps you have a good attitude when you are faced with difficult challenges?

ASSET CATEGORIES: Support, Empowerment, Constructive Use of Time, Commitment to Learning, Social Competencies, Positive Identity

Balloon Stomp

TIME
10–15 minutes

SUPPLIES

- A balloon for every person, plus a few spare balloons
- String
- Scissors

PREP Cut an 18-inch piece of string for each player

THE GAME Let the players blow up the balloons and help them tie them. Use the string pieces to tie a balloon to each player's ankle. When the game leader says "Go," players should try to stomp on other players' balloons while simultaneously guarding their own balloons. A player whose balloon is popped should join the game leader on the sidelines to watch the fun. The last child with a full balloon wins!

GOING DEEPER

- Was it harder to stomp other balloons or to keep your balloon safe?
- What is something you want to protect and keep safe in your life? (Prompt with ideas: character, reputation, dreams, goals, self, etc.)
- What can you do to protect yourself against being stomped on?

- It's easy to get a reputation for what you do. What are some "stomper" actions that lead to a bad reputation (gossiping, bullying, etc.)?

- What are some "protector" actions that do contribute to a good reputation (helping others, etc.)?

- How can you achieve and keep a good reputation?

- What can you do if you see someone stomping on another person's character or even physically threatening that person?

ASSET CATEGORIES: Empowerment, Boundaries and Expectations, Social Competencies, Positive Identity

The Entertainment Committee

TIME
10–15 minutes

THE GAME Ask a few volunteers to leave the room, and tell them their job is to make the audience clap. The volunteers can do whatever they want to get their audience to clap; they just have to make them do it. Separately, you give the audience the instructions to copy every action of the volunteers. This includes repeating what they say. You bring the volunteers back into the room one at a time. When the volunteer leader claps, the audience will also clap, thereby declaring the volunteer to be a winner.

GOING DEEPER

- In part this game is about clues. How can looking for clues help you figure out how to solve or complete tasks or other things in life (such as solving a math problem, fixing a bike, understanding new words, tying your shoes, learning to read a book, resolving conflicts, showing good manners)?

- This game is also about leading and following. Who are some of the people you follow and do what they say?

- What makes them good leaders?

- What do the actions of negative influences or leaders look like?

- What helps you not copy their actions?
- Who copies your actions in your daily life?
- How can you be a positive role model for others?

ASSET CATEGORIES: Empowerment, Commitment to Learning, Social Competencies, Positive Values

Superhero Obstacle Course

TIME
10–15 minutes

SUPPLIES

- Two long, rectangular tables
- Masking tape

PREP Set up the two tables next to each other so that the short ends are adjacent, and then, with tape, mark an area of space by creating a start line on the floor parallel to the long sides of the tables, as well as a corresponding finish line about ten feet away. Finally, on each side of this shared area, there should be a line of tape leading back to the area on the other side of the tables. In effect, this will create a three-stage obstacle course for two teams. The path for each team consists of a table, the shared floor space, and a tightrope back to the beginning.

THE GAME Split the group into two teams. Each team should line up behind one of the tables. Each player is a superhero who must crawl through the "Batcave" (under the tables), get up and somersault or roll away from the bad guys (across a designated playing area marked by tape), and finally walk the spider web tightrope back (placing one foot in front of the other and keeping both feet on the tape) to tag the next person in line. If players "fall" off the tightrope, then they must start over from the beginning of the tightrope.

NOTE If children in your group have not yet developed the coordination to walk a straight line heel to toe, you could allow other kids to help them, or you could allow them to shuffle sideways across the rope.

- Even though you were on teams in this game, facing the obstacle course was an individual effort. What is something that seems like a tough obstacle for you to complete at school, where you have to put in a lot of effort (a particular subject, getting along with someone, being ready to come to school, speaking up in class, etc.)?

- What superhero muscles do you need to work or develop in order to overcome that obstacle?

- Is there a particular obstacle you have right now in other areas of your life? With a friend? At home? In the neighborhood? What is it?

- What do you need to know or do to overcome that obstacle?

- Who are some "allies" who can help you build the skills and confidence you need to meet the challenge?

ASSET CATEGORIES: Support, Empowerment, Constructive Use of Time, Social Competencies, Positive Identity

Snap, Crackle, Pop

TIME
15 minutes

THE GAME Direct players to sit in a circle on the floor. Teach the group the "snap" motion: snap fingers. Choose one person to lead. Tell players they are to snap and say "Snap" one at a time, going clockwise around the circle as fast as possible. Once they've done this successfully, introduce the "crackle" motion: make static sound with mouth while wiggling fingers in the air. When someone says "Crackle," it reverses the direction of the snap. Now, point out a new leader, who can either snap as usual or reverse the direction of play by making the crackling sound and motion back toward the person who passed the "snap" to him. Play continues with players either "snapping" forward or changing the snap's direction by "crackling." When the group has these two motions down, introduce the final element—the "pop." When a player receives the snap or crackle, she can now respond by saying "Pop," and popping out of her seat to find a new place in the circle (someone may need to move over to let her squeeze in). When she sits down, she points to the direction the snap should go. Practice for a few rounds, then start the faster-paced elimination round, in which players who make the wrong move, say the wrong word, or simply act too slowly should step out of the circle and become judges. Play continues until there are two remaining players.

GOING DEEPER

- How did you keep track of all the different moves and what to do?
- How did the elements of time and pressure change the game for you?
- What helps you respond quickly to challenges and make quick decisions under pressure?
- How many of you decided that you would always just snap, instead of crackling or popping? Why did you make that decision? Was it because it was easier or because it was just habit?
- What are things you just do out of habit?
- In what kinds of situations do you feel comfortable trying new things?

ASSET CATEGORIES: Constructive Use of Time, Commitment to Learning, Social Competencies

Double Concentration

TIME
5–10 minutes

SUPPLIES

- Flip chart paper
- Cloth
- Several random objects, such as a toothbrush, a can of soup, a washcloth, a shoe, a writing pen, or a paper clip

THE GAME Make a list of 10 related items on a piece of flip chart paper (for a beach theme, you might list *shovel*, *pail*, *sand*, *ocean*, *pool*, *sunglasses*, *hat*, *lotion*, *bathing suit*, and *waves*). Give players two minutes to memorize the list, then hide the list. Ask them to try to remember as many of the 10 items as they can. Repeat as often as desired. Give a small prize to the ones who remember the most items.

Tangible round: This time hide several objects under a cloth. Let players see what's under the cloth for 30 seconds. Then give them paper and pen and have them record as many objects as they can from memory (45 seconds to write everything down).

GOING DEEPER

- Which method was easier for you, seeing words or seeing objects?

- What did you do to remember as many items as you could on the list? From the visuals?

- What tips could we give others to help them remember all the items?

- What helps you remember to do the things you're asked to do at home?

- In paying attention, you might remember things to ask your friends about the next time you see them. How else can remembering things and concentrating help you in your friendships?

- What is something that requires a lot of concentration on your part?

ASSET CATEGORIES: Support, Commitment to Learning, Positive Values, Social Competencies

Bottle Bowling

TIME
15–20 minutes

SUPPLIES

- 10 empty two-liter bottles

- A soft rubber ball

- Masking tape
- Paper and pen

PREP Set up the bottles in traditional bowling style (four in the back, then three, then two, then one), and mark the start line with masking tape.

THE GAME Divide players into two equally numbered groups. Have each group line up in a "bowling lane." Let players take turns rolling the ball to knock down the pins. Let children take turns setting up the pins between players' turns.

GOING DEEPER #1:

- What is the object of bowling?
- What does it take to knock down all the pins?

For the next round of bowling, let each person write down his goals, tape them to one of the pins, and play again. Before each player rolls the ball, ask him to think about one thing he can do this week to take a step toward "knocking out" that goal, then bowl his ball. That's the commitment roll. Give high fives to each player for taking the steps.

GOING DEEPER #2:

- What are some of the goals you have?
- What can you do to "knock out" those goals? Are there individual steps you need to take to make it happen?
- What helps you stay focused on your goal?
- Who is someone who "high fives" your efforts and cheers you on?

ASSET CATEGORIES: Support, Empowerment, Boundaries and Expectations, Social Competencies, Positive Identity

TEAM CHALLENGES

Alphabet Scavenger Hunt

TIME
5–10 minutes

SUPPLIES

- Arbitrary items from players' bags or desks, or from around the room
- pen and paper to tally score

THE GAME Break the group into teams of four to six players. Tell them that you are going to ask for items based on random letters of the alphabet that you call out. The first player to bring up the item that fits gets a point for her team. For example, if you ask for a *C* item, a team might bring up a tube of ChapStick; if you ask for an *N* item, someone might bring up a nickel or a notebook. The team with the most points at the end wins.

GOING DEEPER

- What is another way we could have played this game?
- What if we had played this individually instead of as teams? How do you think the game would have been different?
- What are some things that you do in everyday life that work better when you do them with others instead of by yourself?
- Did you ever have trouble finding something to match one of the letters?
- Sometimes we don't have everything we need. When you come up short and don't have the right answer or right "stuff" in life, how do you respond?

ASSET CATEGORIES: Support, Empowerment, Positive Values, Social Competencies, Positive Identity

Coin Spellers

TIME

10–15 minutes

SUPPLIES

- A small container of approximately 50 pennies (or rocks, buttons, etc.) for every small group of four or five
- Chalkboard and a piece of chalk, or flip chart paper and a marker

THE GAME Form small groups of four or five players. Read aloud one of the word puzzles (see examples below). The teams will confer among themselves to determine the correct answer, and then they will quickly spell out their one-word answer with their pennies, arranging them in lines that form the shapes of the letters in the word. When they have created the word with their coins, they should raise their hands and yell "Coin Spellers!" Check their answers. Award five points to the first team that answered correctly. Repeat this process for each of the puzzles. The overall point winners claim the prize.

Sample word puzzles:

1. A person who tells the truth is known for being ___. This word starts with the eighth letter in the alphabet. (Honest)

2. What you show when you give someone a hug. This word rhymes with *dove*. (Love)

3. A person who follows the rules of the game plays ___. This word rhymes with *square*. (Fair)

4. You should always treat yourself, others, and other people's things with _____. This word starts with the letter of the alphabet that comes after the letter *Q*. (Respect)

5. If somebody does something bad to you and you don't deserve it, the right thing to do is to ___ them. The first part of the word sounds like the number that comes after three. (Forgive)

6. You shouldn't _____ things from other people without asking. This word rhymes with *rake*. (Take)

7. The opposite of selfishly keeping something just for yourself, like cookies, is to _____ it with others. This word rhymes with *bear*. (Share)

8. If you _____ someone, it means you feel safe with that person and believe that he or she will do the right thing. This word rhymes with *dust* and is a value that is important in friendships. (Trust)

9. This short word means thoughtful, and rhymes with *mind*. (Kind)

10. This word rhymes with *royal* and is often used to describe a dog's devotion to its owner. (Loyal)

GOING DEEPER

- How did your teams work together to solve the puzzles and spell the words?

- How can you support one another through other difficult tasks and challenges?

- Did you notice anything similar about the various words?

- What values are important to you?

- What is one value that is hard for you to practice?

- How can you help one another stay true to your values?

ASSET CATEGORIES: Support, Empowerment, Social Competencies, Positive Values

Build a Tower

TIME
12–15 minutes

SUPPLIES

- Four to five stacks of newspaper (one section of the Sunday paper per team of five should be enough)

- Five rolls of masking tape

THE GAME Break the group into teams of five. Give each team a stack of newspapers and one roll of masking tape. Tell them that their job is to build the highest freestanding tower possible within five minutes, using only newspaper and masking tape. Let them have two minutes to plan. When the time is up, give five minutes for teams to build their towers. If more time is needed, allow it. When time is up, determine the highest tower and applaud the winning team. Also note the variety of towers and what makes each unique.

NOTE To keep this game even more inexpensive, limit each team to two strips of masking tape, each three to five feet long.

GOING DEEPER

- Was everyone involved in the planning and building of the tower? What roles did everyone take on?

- Did you have a plan? Did you try different things just to see what would work (trial and error)? Or did you say, "Let's just build it and see what happens"?

- What was the key for creating a tower that would stand?

- Foundations are important. What makes a good base for a friendship?

- What can you do to support others the rest of this day?

- You built a tower with very few resources. Just two supplies. What are some things you can do for fun that don't take a lot of money or supplies?

- Building the tower took teamwork and creativity. What is one way that you are creative?

- Your goal was to build a high tower. What are some other goals that our group might work toward this year?

ASSET CATEGORIES: Support, Empowerment, Constructive Use of Time, Social Competencies, Positive Identity

High Speed

TIME
10–15 minutes

SUPPLIES

- A squishy or spongy ball that is easy to grab and hold

THE GAME Place the ball in the middle of the playing area. Divide players into two even teams. Have teams face each other some 10–20 feet apart with the ball halfway between them. Starting at one end of each line, have players count themselves off from one to whatever number the last person happens to be. Tell players to remember their individual number. You, as the game leader, will call out a number or group of numbers (one, four, all even, all odd, seven, etc.). Whatever that number is, the player from each team who has that number should race to the middle, try to grab the ball, and race back to her or his team. The player who doesn't get there first can try to tag the other player *before* that person gets back to the line. If the player with the ball is successfully tagged, the ball has to go to the tagging player.

If more than one player from a team is called to the middle, these teammates should not try to tag each other. A player cannot pass the ball, but teammates called into the middle can try to stand in the way of opponents, to try to prevent them from tagging the ball carrier. At the end of the round, the player with the ball sets it back in the middle of the playing area. The next round begins when you call out a new number or group of numbers.

Play a few rounds. You, your helpers, or the teams themselves can keep track of winning rounds if desired. After players have the hang of it, spice things up by having the lines mix up their standing order so that they're not sequential. Play a few more rounds. Next, tell players that since they're doing so well, it's time to take the game up a notch and they are now going to participate in some Challengers Rounds. Call out some math problems ($7 - 3$ or $4 + 1$ or 2×2), and watch as teams figure out the answer and race to claim their prize.

GOING DEEPER

- Each of us has different gifts and we will shine at different times. What is a talent or gift you have?

- What is a talent or skill you would like to further develop?

- Did snagging the prize in the middle motivate you? What about the challenge of the math problem?

- In both cases, you worked really hard to finish but different gifts were needed. Can you think of tasks in your life that you have to use both physical strength and your thinking cap to finish? What are they?

- You worked hard and ran quickly to gain the prize in the middle. What is something in your life that you work really hard to gain? Why is it so important to you?

ASSET CATEGORIES: Constructive Use of Time, Commitment to Learning, Social Competencies, Positive Identity

Mini-Tech Hunt

This game is recommended for grades 3 and up.

TIME
10–15 minutes

SUPPLIES

- One computer with Internet access for each group of four to six

If computers are not available, the following supplies could be used instead: a calculator, an atlas, an encyclopedia, a watch or clock, a calendar, and a large box of Crayola crayons.

THE GAME Divide the group into teams of four to six. Call out various items from the following list for team members to find. The information must come from the computer. The player who finds the information first gets a point for that team. The team with the most points wins.

- How many miles are between Los Angeles, California, and Washington, D.C.?

- What is one of the interstate highways that goes through Nashville, Tennessee?
- What day of the week is July 21 this year?
- What would be a 15 percent tip on a $20 bill?
- What time is it in Sydney, Australia, right now?
- How long does it take you to sing "The Alphabet Song"?
- What is 150×15?
- What does a kangaroo eat?
- What is the name of the largest type of shark?
- What is one of Crayola's fun names for the color red?
- What is the capital of Brazil?
- How many colors are in the Swedish flag?

GOING DEEPER

- How did everyone contribute to the hunt?
- Was there something asked for in this hunt that some or all in your group didn't know how to find? If so, how did you find it?
- When you don't know how to do something in school or at home, what do you do to learn how to do it? Do you ask for help? Read up on it?
- Did you discover a new resource in this hunt that you'll want to look at again?
- In many ways, this game is about combining fun with learning. What can you do to make learning fun?

ASSET CATEGORIES: Support, Empowerment, Commitment to Learning, Social Competencies

Tiddly Buttons

TIME
10–15 minutes

SUPPLIES

- A handful of large and small buttons
- Sidewalk chalk (for an outdoor play area) or a marker, poster board, and masking tape (for indoor playtime)

PREP Draw a 20-inch-diameter target with sidewalk chalk, or draw on a poster board with a marker (you may wish to tape the poster board to the floor). Label the three circles of the target with three numbers: the inner circle (5), the middle circle (3), the outside ring (1). Mark a starting point on the ground for the players to place their small buttons behind—approximately 5 inches from the outside circle.

THE GAME Divide the group into four teams and position them around the tiddly target. Each team nominates one representative to shoot at the target. Each of these starting players should place a small button on the starting point, then use a large button to shoot the small button toward the targets. (When you use the large button to press down on the back edge of the small button, you can shoot the button forward.) Each team should tally its points earned (five points for the inner circle, three points for the middle circle, and one point for the outside circle), and send up another representative to shoot at the target. The team with the most points wins.

GOING DEEPER

- This game requires careful work and a lot of accuracy. How important is accuracy in other things that you do? Schoolwork? Sports? Hobbies? Chores?
- What happens when your work is sloppy instead of accurate?
- Do you ever have to do your tasks over because they were sloppy?
- What is one way that you can work on tasks carefully, neatly, and accurately this week, giving them your very best the first time you do them?

- What is the benefit of giving the things you do your best effort every time?
- How does it make you feel when you do something really well?

ASSET CATEGORIES: Support, Boundaries and Expectations, Commitment to Learning, Social Competencies, Positive Identity

Blind Balance

TIME
10–15 minutes

SUPPLIES
- Three to four blindfolds (one per team)
- Three to four ropes of equal length (approximately 12 feet each)

PREP Lay the ropes on the ground in straight lines, three feet apart and parallel to each other in the playing area.

THE GAME Divide the group into three or four teams and line up each team at the end of a rope. Players should take their shoes off and put them aside. Blindfold the first person in each line. Players should balance on the rope, walking blindly to the end by feeling the rope with their bare feet. If they "fall off" the rope (fail to touch it during a step), they must start over at the beginning of the rope (they can peek out from their blindfolds while they are walking back to the start). When players reach the end of their ropes, they should take their blindfolds off and carry them to the next teammate in line. The first team that has everyone successfully balanced across the rope wins.

NOTE If children in your group have not yet developed the coordination to walk a straight line heel to toe, you could allow them to choose other kids to help them, or you could allow them to shuffle sideways across the rope.

GOING DEEPER
- How did you keep your balance on the rope? What was your secret?

- Did you help one another with tips for keeping your balance?

- Balancing takes a lot of focus. How do you stay focused on your projects, whether you are doing homework, practicing a musical instrument, or painting a picture?

- It's especially hard to stay focused when there are a lot of distractions, such as a noisy television or a cheering crowd. How do you keep your mind on the task at hand when there are distractions around you?

- How can you support one another when you face future tasks that require tricky balance and focus?

ASSET CATEGORIES: Support, Boundaries and Expectations, Social Competencies, Positive Identity

Beach Ball Volley

TIME
5–10 minutes

SUPPLIES
- One beach ball
- Masking tape

THE GAME Divide the group into two teams. Using masking tape, mark a dividing line between the two teams. Have the teams sit on the floor on their side of the line (it doesn't matter how close or far from the line they are; teams will adjust as play proceeds). The challenge is for the group to keep the ball up in the air for 25 volleys without letting it drop. (You can have the group set a goal or you can set a number to challenge them. If it's reached, the group can set a new goal.) The goal is to keep the beach ball up *and* to volley it back and forth between sides. Each player should hit it to another player; a player can only hit it twice in a row. If an individual player hits it three times in a row, then an out is called. A team can only hit the ball a maximum of five times on its side of the line. Teams must try to volley it to each other. If a team hits it more than five times on its side of the line before the ball passes over the line, then an out is called. A ball is also out if it hits the wall or the floor. When outs are called, play must begin again.

GOING DEEPER

- If you were giving someone else the secrets for making this game work, what would they be?
- How many teams were there—*really*—in this game? Can you describe another experience where you thought there were multiple teams, but really you were all working toward the same goal as one team?
- For us as a group, how important are teamwork, communication, and cheering? What about at home, at school, or in the neighborhood?
- What can you do personally to improve your own skills in these three areas?
- How can we be sure to keep these actions in mind as we work together as a group?

ASSET CATEGORIES: Support, Empowerment, Social Competencies, Positive Identity

TIME
15–20 minutes

SUPPLIES

- 16 paper plates
- Marker
- Tape
- Dice
- Scrap paper and a pencil

PREP Set up 16 paper plates in a circle to represent a racetrack. On 7 of the plates, write directional messages to the driving team on the underside of the plates (messages are included below), and mark the topside of those plates with a star. Do not mark stars on the plates without messages. Mix the starred plates randomly among the plain ones. Use tape to denote the starting line and finish line.

Directional message examples to include on plates:

Need gas. Crawl back two spaces.

Turbo boost. Jump forward three spaces.

Rev engine. Make "vroom" car noises and move ahead one space.

Flat tire. Crabwalk back four spaces.

Great start. Speed-walk ahead four spaces.

Green light. Go forward two spaces.

Pothole. Move back one space.

THE GAME Set the stage by telling the group that what they see before them is a racetrack made up of plates. Split the group into driving teams of two—one driver and one navigator. Each team will go around the racetrack separately—there will be only one team on the track at a time. The team-mates should stand at the start line and roll a die. If they roll a three, the driver and the navigator should drive (scoot) forward three plates and sit together in their imaginary race car on either side of the plate. If they land on a space with a star, then the navigator should read the directions to the driver. They then both follow the new instructions. The navigator should also use pencil and paper (racetrack log) to keep track of the number of die rolls it takes them to go around the racetrack. The team that uses the few-est rolls to get around the track wins the race.

NOTE This game works best with fewer than 15 players. Otherwise, make two racetracks or consider having three players per car. In this situation, there should be a driver, a die roller, and a navigator. The die roller can roll the die and tell the navigator the number to record. At the end of their run, they should add up their rolls together as a team.

GOING DEEPER

- You moved forward when things went well. You moved back when things weren't going so well. Sometimes things seem to really go your way. How have you been lucky in your life? What are the really good things in your life that you appreciate? What do you do with those blessings and gifts?

- Sometimes it seems like you are unlucky and bad things happen or things are always going wrong. In your recent experience, what kinds of things have gone wrong?

- Not all bad things that happen are due to bad luck. Sometimes un-fortunate things happen because we haven't done our part, like when a car runs out of gas. When have you had something go wrong because you forgot to do your part?

- Sometimes there are simply bumps in the road that we have to work around—*challenges*. How do you handle the challenges that crop up in life?

- What is a challenge you're facing right now that is hard for you? How can you respond to it so that the challenge doesn't get the best of you?

ASSET CATEGORIES: Support, Empowerment, Boundaries and Expectations, Positive Values, Social Competencies, Positive Identity

Flight School

TIME
20 minutes

SUPPLIES

- One yardstick or stick
- At least one hard-boiled or plastic egg per team of four to six (for indoor play) or three to four raw eggs per team (for outdoor play)
- Spoons
- A pack of 10–12 eight-inch balloons

PREP Blow up the balloons and tie them.

THE GAME Divide your group into teams of four to six players each. Teams will compete to see who has the best pilots. There are four categories in the competition:

1. **Takeoff:** Players line up in ascending order, with the first player taking the "low" position and lying on the ground; the last player stands on tiptoes with arms reaching toward the sky. All other players are staggered to make one smooth imaginary line going up and down between the lowest and highest spots. The first team to make a smooth line wins the "takeoff award."

2. **Smooth flying:** Teams should line up for a relay. Each team member must take a turn to balance an egg on a spoon from the starting line to a marked turning point, and back to tag the next player. If she drops the egg, she must start again. The first team to finish successfully wins the "smooth flying award."

3. **Maneuvering bad weather:** Teams should each gather in a circle. The teams will compete one at a time. You will toss balloons into the center of the group one by one, and the group needs to juggle the balloons by tapping them up into the air in one hit without catching them. The game leader should announce "one," "two," "three" . . . so the team knows how many balloons they are juggling. The team that can juggle the most balloons without dropping one wins the award for "maneuvering bad weather."

4. **Landing:** The game leader and an assistant should hold a yardstick at shoulder level to represent the limbo bar. Players should line up behind the limbo bar and attempt to go under it with their bellies facing the bar and only their feet touching the floor. (Players cannot duck and run under—they must go limbo style.) Any player who touches the limbo bar while going under it is out. When the entire group has attempted to pass under the limbo bar, the game leader should lower the bar a few inches. The last player to successfully pass under the limbo bar at its lowest is the winner. The team represented by the best limbo competitor wins the "landing award."

Give awards in each category, as well as an overall "flight school award" to the team winning the most categories.

GOING DEEPER

- This game required each of us to use our unique skills and talents. What are some of the factors that make each of us special? Why is our group stronger because we are each unique?

- Each of our minds is also unique. Share some examples of how you think differently. Why is it good that we have different kinds of thinkers in our group?

- In real life, what kinds of challenges do you face individually or as a group? How do you respond to those challenges? How would you like to respond to challenges in the future?

- Your challenge in this game was to be the best team of pilots. How did you work together to be the best?

- In what parts of your life do you want to be the best you can be?

- How are you working toward being your best in those areas?

ASSET CATEGORIES: Support, Empowerment, Boundaries and Expectations, Social Competencies, Positive Identity

Walk across the Country

TIME
10–15 minutes

SUPPLIES

- Masking tape
- Permanent marker
- List of the states or provinces
- Possibly index cards
- A map of your country, continent, or region (for reference)

PREP Make sure you have enough masking tape to make 50 small pieces. If your country is the United States, write one state's abbreviation on each piece of masking tape. Count the number of players in your group and determine whether players will need to use one shoe or both shoes to represent each of the various states. If you have fewer than 25 players, you can use index cards to capture the remaining states (one per card).

THE GAME Have players take off their shoes and label each shoe with a state. Shuffle the shoes into a pile in the middle of the game area. Set the timer and see how quickly the group can create a map of the country using their shoe states. The completed puzzle won't have the *shape* of the country, but it will have the states (shoes) in the proper places (for the United States, California will be to the far left with Arizona and New Mexico going to the right across the bottom of the puzzle). When players are finished, jumble up the shoes and see if the group can rebuild the map in a shorter period of time.

NOTE You can easily adapt this game to represent Canada, Europe, or other geographical areas for a more global game. Or, for younger children, simply use letters of the alphabet on the shoes, and ask them to put the shoes in alphabetical order. You could also use numbers for the shoes, and ask children to put all the shoes in numerical order.

GOING DEEPER

- How did it feel to have the support of the group as you worked together to accomplish the task?
- How did your group's time change from one game to the next? Why did it change?
- Why is it important to know where places are located?
- Which location would you like to visit one day?
- Do you know any cool facts about any of these places?

ASSET CATEGORIES: Support, Empowerment, Commitment to Learning, Social Competencies

All Toss

TIME

12–20 minutes

SUPPLIES

- A throwable object for each person (a ball, a paper wad, a piece of candy, etc.)

THE GAME Each of the players is given a throwable object, and they begin by standing in a circle (though this formation will quickly disperse). All players set down their objects, except for one person you choose to be the first thrower. On the count of three, that person throws her or his object high into the air—without aiming for any other player—and someone else attempts to catch it. If it is caught, you, as the game leader, should select another person to pick up an object. At the count of three, both of the players holding objects throw them up into the air, and the others attempt to catch them before they hit the ground. If both objects are caught, indicate a third person to pick up an object and throw it into the air on the count of three. Keep repeating the process. If an object hits the ground without being caught, then that object is taken out of play. In general, if all the thrown objects are caught, one object is added each round. The goal is to work up to having all of the objects thrown and caught at once.

There are only two rules:

1. A thrower cannot throw either to herself or to the person next to her.

2. All objects in play must be thrown simultaneously.

NOTE The game can be varied so that you, the game leader, personally throw all the new objects to enter each successful round, or the game can be designed to double the number of objects that are thrown in each round, which would help to teach math skills. Using objects of varying shape and weight adds to the challenge.

GOING DEEPER

- What did you try first to be successful?

- What was the difference between your first few attempts and your last ones? What did you change? Why was it necessary to change your methods?

- Imagine that you had not changed anything from your first attempt. What do you think the result would have been?

- In this game, we all had a part to play. What are some of the ways each of you has contributed to our group?

- At the end of the game, we were able to keep up _____ (fill in the number) objects. What are some of the things we have been able to accomplish as a group? Maybe you didn't even think we'd be able to do them.

ASSET CATEGORIES: Support, Empowerment, Boundaries and Expectations, Social Competencies, Positive Identity

Celebrations

Play keeps us vital and alive. It gives us an enthusiasm for life that is irreplaceable. Without it, life just doesn't taste good.
—**LUCIA CAPACCHIONE,** art therapist, author

When it comes to celebrating life, it is perhaps *our* turn to take lessons from children. Children seem to have a natural propensity to laugh, to live freely in the moment with pure joy, pleasure, and even abandonment. But somewhere along the way, if one is not careful, they (and we) "unlearn" how to play and celebrate life's gifts, joys, and moments. Rather, the opposite should hold true and the act of celebrating (moments or milestones) should be encouraged as a gift to be embraced and used throughout our lives. It is in the practice of celebrating that we hold on to joy and laughter; it is in this act of playfulness that we renew the strength of our spirits and find courage to meet challenges.

Psychologist Penelope Leach said that "for a small child there is no division between playing and learning; between the things he or she does 'just for fun' and things that are 'educational.' The child learns while living and any part of living that is enjoyable is also play." Celebrating is about noting that which is good in life.

The following games are intended to remind us to create celebratory moments along the way as the children grow individually and as a group. They range in intensity from quiet and reflective to artsy and creative to high movement. No matter which one you choose, keep celebrating and feeding into your group's spirit the sense of the goodness of life.

Thumbkins Appreciation

TIME
8–12 minutes

SUPPLIES

- Slips of paper
- Ink pads with washable ink
- 8½" × 11" paper
- Washable markers

Make sure you have access to soap and water so children can wash their hands. Otherwise consider using baby wipes.

THE GAME Have players write their names on slips of paper. Collect the papers and let each person draw a name from your hand. Players who draw their own names should return them to pull another one. Tell the group that they're going to create an appreciation card for the person whose name they drew.

Have each person take an 8½" × 11" paper and fold it in half. On the front, have everyone use the ink pads to make a thumbprint on the middle of the card and write "You are thumb-body special" above or beneath it. They can then decorate their thumbkin art and turn it into a smiley face, person, or flower or whatever they want.

On the inside they should write down some of the things that make the person whose name they drew special and what they like about that person. It could be how she's always smiling, the first one to help, or good at math. Allow five minutes for everyone to create a card. When they're done, players can distribute their cards; allow time for everyone to look at the "gifts" and express appreciation to one another.

GOING DEEPER

- How did it feel to praise someone else? How did it feel to receive a special drawing from someone else?

- How did it feel to discover what someone else admires about you? What were some of the things that person likes about you?

- How does it feel when others point out the good in you? Does it make you want to be a better person?

- Is pointing out what others do well a natural part of our conversations? Why or why not?

- How does praising and sharing good things affect us as a group? How does it make us feel about each other? How does it make our environment more pleasant?

- If you want, go around the circle and ask for a few more comments about what makes each person "thumb-body special."

Challenge the group to praise and show their appreciation for one another throughout the week. Brainstorm ways that they can do that for the week.

ADAPTATION Have participants make a thumbprint on the middle of a card and add the wording "I am thumb-body special" on the paper. Let them complete their picture however they desire but also illustrate by words or pictures one or two things that make them special. Let each player share.

GOING DEEPER FOR THE ADAPTATION

- Was it difficult or easy to think of good things about yourself?

- What are some of the things that make you special?

- What are some of the good things about you that others have pointed out?

- What is a quality you hope to develop further?

ASSET CATEGORIES: Support, Empowerment, Constructive Use of Time, Positive Values, Social Competencies, Positive Identity

Freeze Frame

TIME
10–15 minutes

SUPPLIES

- Music and music player

THE GAME This game should be played in a large open area. Tell players that the question of the day for them to ponder during this activity is "What is one thing you want to celebrate?" It could be something they like about the group, something they've done that they're proud of, a good grade they earned, a good decision they made, a task they've accomplished, or any other positive quality or achievement.

Select one person to be the DJ. The DJ turns away from all the other players and starts the music. Everyone begins dancing freestyle, until the DJ stops the music, calls out "Freeze Frame," and turns quickly to look at the dancers. Everyone freezes mid–dance move. If the DJ sees anyone moving, then that dancer must share her answer to the question, then take a seat (though she can still dance in place while she is seated). Start the music and continue play until all dancers have shared during their turn at Freeze Frame. *Or,* if time is an issue, have the DJ call out "Freeze Frame" six different times. At that point, any remaining dancers simply rotate taking turns sharing their answer to the Freeze Frame question.

GOING DEEPER

- Do you think music helped create a celebratory mood? How or how not?

- What about dancing? How does that contribute to celebrations?

- What are other ways we could celebrate the good things that happen in our lives?

- What are some of the ways you know that other cultures celebrate fun events?

- What memories do you want to "freeze" in your mind (remember) with regard to our group and our time together?

- What are some things we could do to capture those memories so that we don't forget? (This might lead into a project idea, for instance, creating a scrapbook, everyone writing or drawing in a journal, etc.)

ASSET CATEGORIES: Support, Empowerment, Constructive Use of Time, Social Competencies, Positive Identity

Canvas Word Art

TIME
12–15 minutes

SUPPLIES
- Canvas material cut into strips (12 inches long, 4–5 inches wide)
- Paint or markers
- Table space for work

THE GAME Give each player a canvas strip along with paints or markers. Say that each person should create a word cluster, a motto, or a picture to express the strengths and gifts of the group. What are some of the good things about this group? What has been a gift of being part of this group? What is something they love about this group?

Give them five to eight minutes to create their masterpiece reflections. After everyone has finished, collect all the pieces. (If you have used paint, you'll need to allow a few hours of drying time.) Ask the group to gather in a circle. Go around and have each player take one of the strips of canvas from you. It's okay if they get their own (unless they really don't want their own, then let them select a different one). Go around the circle and have all players share out loud the word cluster or motto from the strip they randomly pulled out of the pile. There should be no talking as each person takes a turn sharing.

Tell players that they get to take home and keep their gifts. Encourage them to display their canvases somewhere where they can see them to remember the gift of being part of this group.

NOTE We have found that children enjoy this feeling of giving, and due to the limited time for work, they usually do not get too attached to their own artwork. But if you sense that this is an issue, you could allow them to trade back for their own projects at the end.

GOING DEEPER

- What were some of the things that were said that you really liked? Why did that strike you?

- As you listened to the various strengths that were shared, did other things come to mind? Did you remember other good times in this group or things you appreciate? What were they?

- What's the one thing you hope everyone remembers about this group?

ASSET CATEGORIES: Support, Empowerment, Boundaries and Expectations, Constructive Use of Time, Social Competencies, Positive Identity

This game is recommended for grades 3 and up.

TIME
10–15 minutes

SUPPLIES

- Recycled colored paper cut into various shapes and sizes (generally about four to six inches across and enough for there to be two or three shapes per player)

- Kaleidoscope (optional)

THE GAME Lay out a large assortment of recycled colored paper in various shapes and sizes. Stand in a circle around the colors. Tell the group that all the mixed, swirled colors represent a kaleidoscope. (If the players are unfamiliar with kaleidoscopes, have an actual one on hand to show them.) Invite each person to think about which piece of the kaleidoscope best represents her or his day-to-day contribution to the group—her energy, her ideas, his smile, his helpfulness, and so on. After a couple of minutes, ask players to point to the part of the kaleidoscope that best represents them and share how it represents their contribution to the group. After everyone has shared, walk as a group around the kaleidoscope, looking at it from various angles. Point out to the group that it takes all the different individual pieces to make up the whole kaleidoscope, just as it takes all their contributions to make up the group's beauty and strength.

NOTE For groups with limited attention spans, encourage participants to limit their responses about how they contribute to four or five words in order to keep the pace of the activity moving quickly. If your group is larger than 12, you might consider having two kaleidoscope groups so that the game doesn't stretch to be too long.

GOING DEEPER

- Was it easy or hard to think of your contributions to this group in terms of color and shapes?

- How have our individual contributions added to the group as a whole? What are some of our group's strengths?

- How are we stronger and more beautiful when we work together?

- With a kaleidoscope, the pieces can move around and create different pictures. How have we been able to "move around" and be flexible when we were working together?

- Kaleidoscopes create many pictures. What are some of the "pictures" (memories) we've created that you want to remember?

- What are some of the things we want to create as we go forward? What is a mark we want to leave behind?

ASSET CATEGORIES: Support, Constructive Use of Time, Social Competencies, Positive Identity

Balloon Skipping

10–15 minutes

SUPPLIES

- Balloons (one per team)

THE GAME This is a game that focuses on setting, accomplishing, and celebrating a team goal. Split the group into teams of six to eight players. Have them stand in separate lines, far enough apart so that their fingertips touch when their arms are outstretched. Blow up and tie one balloon for each team. Player 1 will tap the balloon to player 2, who taps the balloon—without holding it—to player 3. Challenge the teams to see how far they can "skip" the balloon along the line without catching the balloon. If the balloon falls to the ground or the players in line move out of formation, the team must start over. The team with the most consecutive skips (no drops or getting out of place) in a set period of time is designated the Overall Longest Skipper Extraordinaires; teams that successfully skip the balloon along their entire line are Skipping Experts. If all the teams succeed at this challenge quickly, then make the teams bigger and see how far they can skip the balloons. Continue to build until you have one big team.

GOING DEEPER

- How did you encourage and help each other be successful?

- Have you ever skipped rocks on a lake or pond? If so, what is the trick to making the rock skip over the water?

- When you are skipping rocks, you often set a goal of how many skips you'll do and work toward that. What are some goals you have set personally? How successful are you right now in working toward those goals?

- What are some things we have set out to do as a group? Where have we "skipped rocks" successfully and met our goals?

- Where have we done more than we thought we would or could?

- What is something we want to work toward next? What will it take for us to be successful in "skipping" that rock? What do we need to be successful?

ASSET CATEGORIES: Support, Empowerment, Boundaries and Expectations, Social Competencies, Positive Identity

Royal Affirmations

TIME
10–20 minutes

SUPPLIES
- Small pieces of scrap paper
- A pen for each person
- A chair to serve as a "throne" for the Royal Person of Honor to sit on, as well as a crown, sash, and other things royalty carry or wear (optional)

THE GAME Give participants scrap paper and pens. Have one person sit in the middle of the group on the "throne." This individual is to be considered the Royal Person of Honor, and the other players are her or his admirers. After the Royal Person of Honor is seated, encourage the others to write down something they appreciate or admire about her or him. Challenge the group to think about the person's character, personality, actions, and words in order to honor her or him, everything from "You always encourage me" to "I love your ready smile and quick wit" to "You are always the first to jump in and volunteer." When all players are finished, they should deliver their messages to you, the game leader. You should then select a Town Crier to read aloud all the positive messages. Rotate Royal Persons of Honor and Town Criers and play as long as time permits.

NOTE This game can be led in two ways. It's your choice depending on which skill set you want to emphasize in your group *and* depending on the comfort level of your group. The basic goal is to share things that the children appreciate about one another. The decision comes when it's time to read all the messages out loud—you can have a Town Crier read all the messages that children write about a particular person. Or, the Royal Person of Honor can read aloud all the things people had to say about her or him. This second choice might be a higher risk. It's not easy for us to claim our own gifts, but it's an important skill to be able to practice verbalizing positives about ourselves. So if your group can handle it and you want to help your children practice verbalizing their own worth, then simply leave the Town Crier out of the picture and adjust the wording of the Going Deeper questions as needed.

You may want to carry out this activity over a few sessions should time be a factor.

ALTERNATE ENDING If you want to create a memoir for the Royal Person of Honor to take home, let players use sticky notes and post their encouraging words on a poster board, a piece of flip chart paper, or a piece of cardboard. You could even decorate the poster boards with a royal symbol, such as a crown, or the words "You Are a Royal Person of Honor."

GOING DEEPER

- Raise your hand if you were in the middle as the Royal Person of Honor: How did it feel to hear all the nice things that other people like about you?

- How often do we take the time to tell others what makes them special to us?

- How often do we take the time to claim our own gifts and talents?

- How important is it to have good self-esteem?

- What can you do to build your own sense of positive identity? (One idea to share is to write down affirmations about yourself, post them where you can see them, and read them at least once each day.)

Go around the group and have individuals share one thing they want to celebrate about themselves (or about the group).

ASSET CATEGORIES: Support, Boundaries and Expectations, Positive Values, Social Competencies, Positive Identity

Celebration Meter

TIME
8–12 minutes

THE GAME Have the group split into pairs. Ask players to share the biggest thing they want to celebrate about their day (it could be something from school or home, or their time in the group—how it worked well together, what the team accomplished, etc.). Give them three minutes to come up with a word, expression, or motion to reflect their celebration meter. Go around the circle letting each team demonstrate its celebration meter and what it's celebrating.

GOING DEEPER

- Is there a celebration moment that you would like to ask more about?
- Celebrating is a good thing. What kinds of things does our community celebrate?
- Have you ever been part of a group (a sports team, a club, or your family) that enjoys celebrating? What did you celebrate? How did you celebrate?
- What is your favorite way to celebrate?
- What are the things that mean a lot to you personally that you like to celebrate?
- What is something you think our group should celebrate? What are some of the things we have done well, either as a group or just someone in the group?

Challenge the group to look for little things as well as big things to celebrate each day.

ASSET CATEGORIES: Support, Boundaries and Expectations, Positive Values, Social Competencies, Positive Identity

Opposite Ends

Recommended for grades 3 and up.

TIME
5–10 minutes

THE GAME Have participants vote with their feet by walking to stand on the side of the room that best fits their response to the question asked. Pairings include "opposites." Ask one or two volunteers to share why they picked the side of the room they did. Affirm that there is no right or wrong answer.

Sample questions:

Was your experience (in this activity, class, group meeting) more like peanut butter or jelly? Why?

Was this experience more like an animal or a plant? Why?

Was our time together more like a day at the zoo or a day in a museum? Why?

Is our group more like a rock band or an orchestra? Why?

Is our group salty or sweet? Why?

NOTE This game is designed to be used after a group project or group experience. It helps the groups reflect on their time together as they celebrate successes.

GOING DEEPER

- Which pairing of opposites was your favorite?
- What has been your favorite part about being with this group?
- What is one thing you will miss most about being together?
- What is one thing you have learned from being a part of the group?

ASSET CATEGORIES: Support, Empowerment, Social Competencies, Positive Identity

Rainmakers

TIME

5–8 minutes

THE GAME

Demo: As the game leader, you should demonstrate a series of motions while the group is completely silent, watching and listening in a quiet space. Go through each of the following motions, a few seconds per motion before moving on to the next motion: rub your hands together back and forth, tap one index finger on the palm of your other hand, snap your fingers with both hands, then drumroll (tap) both hands on your thighs. Stop and ask the group if they could tell what sound you were trying to make through all the motions. If they say "rain," then affirm their answer. If they don't guess rain, tell them to keep thinking as you continue with round one.

Round one: This time you'll lead them through the same series of motions you just demonstrated. All players will stand in a circle. When you make eye contact with a player, he will start doing the same action that you are doing, such as rubbing his hands together. That player will continue rubbing his hands together until you signal a change in action by making eye contact and modeling the new action. Go around the circle making eye contact with each player, silently signaling the players to mimic your first action of rubbing hands together. When you get all the way around the circle, signal the players one by one to change motions to the index finger tapping on the palm. This same process will continue as you take the players through each motion: rubbing of hands, tapping fingers, snapping fingers, drumroll, and then *reverse* the order—from drumroll to snapping fingers to tapping fingers to rubbing hands to quiet. After going through all the motions, ask the group again, "What sound did we make together?" See if they guess rain. If they don't, then prompt them to think about nature and the sounds they just made.

If time permits, ask the group if anyone would be willing to share a time when he or she has experienced the sounds of a strong thunderstorm. (You might get a wide range of personal experiences that cover everything from being in a car when Mom had to pull over to being on Grandma's back porch to lying in bed with the window open.)

Round two: Ask the group, "What could we do to make this sound more like a thunderstorm?" If they say, "Add thunder," ask them how they could simulate thunder. If they say, "Add lightning," ask them how they could simulate lightning. Then try to make a rainstorm together with the new additions to the "orchestra." Don't forget that you'll need to be the one to cue the thunder and the lightning. (For thunder, you might designate four or five players to jump up and down or stomp their feet. For lightning, you might have a child flick the lights, flash a flashlight, or flick the window shades—whatever will create the best sense of light versus dark.)

NOTE This game is most effective with at least 10 players, and it works well with more than 100 players.

GOING DEEPER

- You did a miracle together—you made rain! Could you have made rain by yourself?

- With just one person doing the actions, how did it sound? When everyone worked together, how did it sound?

- What would have happened if someone didn't follow the game leader's instructions?

- What would have happened if some of us chose not to play, and instead just started talking on the side?

- To be successful in this game, we needed everyone's attention and actions. It took teamwork. What is something we've done really well together as a group?

- How has each of us contributed to the group so far? How can we celebrate our good work?

ASSET CATEGORIES: Support, Empowerment, Boundaries and Expectations, Social Competencies, Positive Identity

Shuffle, Shuffle

TIME
5–8 minutes

PREP Determine an open-ended reflection question that you want every-one to answer, such as "What is the thing you will most remember about today?" or "The one thing I appreciate most about this group is . . ."

THE GAME Gather the players into a circle and have them put their arms around the shoulders of the people to either side. Tell them that you will give the group a shuffling direction to follow. Once the group is going in that direction, any player can say "Stop!" to stop the motion. Once the group stops, the player who said "Stop!" should share her answer to the reflection question.

After she has shared her answer, she will then guide the group regard-ing the direction in which they will shuffle next. For example, she might want the group to now shuffle left or to shuffle "in" (meaning all the play-ers move in toward the center and get really tight), or shuffle "out" (mean-ing players shuffle their feet backward, which will make the circle large and stretch everyone's arms out), or she may want to continue shuffling in the direction they were already going *or* she might get creative and offer up some kind of shuffle off the top of her head (for example, shuffle in and shuffle out or shuffle down).

At her direction, the group will shuffle until the next player signals a stop. Repeat the process—shuffle, stop, answer, give a new shuffle direc-tion, stop, answer, and so on—until everyone has had a chance to share.

Start play by sharing the reflection question for players to answer, and thenshare the four basic shuffle moves—left, right, in, out—and cue the group to shuffle right.

GOING DEEPER questions are not used for this game, as the entire activity is itself a Going Deeper exercise.

ASSET CATEGORIES: Support, Empowerment, Boundaries and Expectations, Social Competencies, Positive Identity

Game Leader's Insight:
Even Breaks Can Be Full of Fun

Play is our brain's favorite way of learning.
—**DIANE ACKERMAN,** American poet and naturalist

There are definitely times when groups need breaks or when breaks just naturally occur in the day. A group might need a physical break, for example, after riding in a van for many hours, or a break presents itself when a group has to walk from one room to another. Sometimes the clock or your agenda will tell you when it's time for a change. The group may send off signals of restlessness or hyperactivity, or you might observe a few looks of boredom or even listlessness.

Whatever the reason for the break, these transitions don't have to be mechanical or stale. Nor do they have to be opportunities for bored young people to discover other ways to entertain themselves and get into trouble. You can make breaks fun by creating chants, cheers, songs, or rituals to while away the time.

We present here just a few ideas to get you thinking about how you can have fun with some natural breaks and also get across a life lesson or two about healthy living. Then, you can continue what you create break after break.

GAMES FOR BREAKS

TIME
15–20 minutes

THE GAME Before starting this game, ask players if they are familiar with the term H_2O. If they are not, briefly explain that this is the chemical abbreviation for water.

Phase 1: Teach this chant to your group: "H! 2! O! H! 2! O! H_2O is the way to go!" (Clap to each letter and maintain that beat for the duration, except for "is the," which is a double beat.)

Phase 2: Talk about the importance of water in having healthy lives.

Phase 3: Designate chant leaders to lead the cheer before water or bathroom breaks or during field trips. It serves as a simple, fun reminder to hydrate and provides an easy opportunity for children to take on leadership roles.

Phase 4: Challenge teams of three players to come up with their own cheer, chant, or skit (your choice) about the importance of water (five to eight minutes to create). Let the teams take turns teaching their chant (or performing their skit) to the rest of the group. This can be done as a complete session in itself or done daily or even weekly to keep the message alive over time.

GOING DEEPER

- How much water do you drink on a regular basis?
- Why do you think we spent time in this game thinking about water?
- Why is water so important?
- What do you think it would be like not to have enough water to meet your needs? How would your life be different without water?
- What can you do to make sure you drink enough water each day?

ASSET CATEGORIES: Constructive Use of Time, Positive Identity, Boundaries and Expectations, Empowerment

Snack Attack

TIME
15–20 minutes

THE GAME This game involves four phases.

Phase 1: Teach this song to your group, to the tune of "It's Raining, It's Pouring" ("It's raining, it's pouring, the old man is snoring; he went to bed and bumped his head, and couldn't get up in the morning"):

> *Let's e-at, let's dri-ink.*
> *On what we must thi-ink.*
> *Veggies a must, fruits a plus,*
> *Water and juice com ple-ete.*

Phase 2: Talk about the importance of healthy snacks in having healthy lives.

Phase 3: Designate chant leaders to lead the cheer before snack breaks. The rhyme serves as a simple, fun reminder to eat healthy snacks and provides an easy opportunity for children to take on leadership during their time with you. You could even invite the children to make up motions to go with the lyrics.

Phase 4: Give the group simple tunes they may know, such as "Twinkle, Twinkle, Little Star" or Barney's song ("I love you, you love me . . ."). Hand out copies of the lyrics. Challenge teams of three to five players to come up with their own songs about the importance of healthy snacks (five to eight minutes to create) using the tune you have provided. Let the teams take turns teaching their song to the rest of the group. (This can be done as a complete session in itself or done daily or even weekly to keep alive the message about the importance of eating healthy snacks instead of food that has no nutritional value.)

GOING DEEPER

- What is your favorite snack?
- What is your favorite fruit? Vegetable?
- What is a vegetable or fruit you haven't tried yet? Why haven't you tried it? What would it take to get you to try it?

- What are good choices you make at home with regard to eating? Do you eat healthy snacks?

- Does your family have a neat way to remind each other to eat healthy food? If not, how can you help be an example at home?

- How can you set an example with your friends for making healthy food choices?

ASSET CATEGORIES: Boundaries and Expectations, Constructive Use of Time, Positive Identity

Alien Dancers

TIME
8–12 minutes

SUPPLIES

- Flip chart paper and markers

PREP Draw arrows representing dance steps on a large piece of flip chart paper. Example: Up, back, right, left, circle right, circle left, wiggle down, wiggle up, clap

THE GAME Tell players that they are a group of beings from a faraway planet coming to Earth to learn how to dance. They will see on the instruction board a series of dance steps that they should follow with the group. Start slow, modeling each move for the group, then slowly speed up the tempo to see how quickly the group can go through the motions. If your group is really advanced, invite them to add their own dance moves, and try the group dance again.

This game can be used as a fun energy break for when you see energy waning, or when players are getting restless. This activity gets them up and moving for a few minutes as a stretch break before going back to work.

GOING DEEPER

- Which combination of steps did you like best? What is your favorite move?

- This game got you moving. What are things you like to do to "move" and play?

- How often do you exercise, run, and play? Weekly? Daily?

- In the game, you were a being from another planet learning something new. Do you ever feel like an alien when you are trying to learn something that feels foreign?

- Who helps you feel more welcome in learning about new things?

- How can you help others feel more comfortable when you know a lot about a subject and they don't?

ASSET CATEGORIES: Empowerment, Constructive Use of Time, Commitment to Learning

GAME TITLE	PAGE	LOCATION			RISK LEVEL			ENERGY LEVEL		SUPPLIES
		INSIDE	OUTSIDE	IN/OUT	LOW	MED	HIGH	SITTING	MOVING	
Birthday Scramble	17			•	•				•	•
Name Song	18			•		•		•		•
Name that Person!	19			•		•		•		
Cartoon Names	20			•	•			•		
Super Names	21			•		•		•		
Mission: Names Ice Breaker	22			•		•			•	•
Who's Coming to Snacks and Play?	23			•	•			•		
Drum Beat Name Game	24			•		•			•	
Rhyming Names	25			•		•		•		
Name Search	26	•			•			•		•
Fill It Up	29			•	•				•	•
Hot Potato Jumble	30			•		•			•	•
Uniquely Me	31			•		•			•	•
Dice Details	32			•		•		•		•
Colorful Characters	33			•		•		•		
Musical Matches	34			•		•			•	•
Nicknames Chronicles	35			•		•		•		
Circle-ups	38			•					•	
Players in the Band	39			•		•			•	•
Singing Partners	39			•		•			•	•
Lollipop Tongues Break Out	40			•	•			•		
Circus Stars	41			•		•			•	•
Choice Picks	41			•	•				•	
Rhyming Partners	42			•	•				•	•
Connections	44			•		•			•	
Conversation Rotations	45			•		•			•	•
Lucky Numbers	46			•		•			•	•
Categorically Speaking	47			•		•		•		•
Color Hunt	49			•	•				•	•
Snowball Conversations	50			•		•				•
Elbow Tag	51			•	•				•	
Loopy Conversations	53			•		•		•		•
Design Your Own Superhero Identity	54			•		•		•		•
Names Stack	55	•			•			•		•
Guess Who	56			•		•		•		•
Just Roll It	58			•		•		•		•
Star Inquirer	59			•		•			•	•

GAME TITLE	PAGE	LOCATION			RISK LEVEL			ENERGY LEVEL		SUPPLIES
		INSIDE	OUTSIDE	IN/OUT	LOW	MED	HIGH	SITTING	MOVING	
Shuffle the Deck	60			•	•				•	•
Guardian Shields	62			•		•		•		•
Connect Four	63			•		•			•	
Fingers Down	64			•		•			•	
Buzzing Bee	68			•	•				•	•
Duck, Duck, Goose	69			•	•				•	
Balloon Cup Race	70		•		•				•	•
Cymbal Crashers	72			•	•				•	•
Puzzle-Piece Pictures	73	•				•			•	•
Puzzle Flips	74	•				•		•		•
Traffic Patrol	75			•	•				•	
Chaos Pass	76			•		•			•	•
Gossip on the Run	77			•		•			•	•
Balloon Ups and Downs	79	•				•			•	
What's In a Look?	81			•	•			•		
Extreme Teams	82			•		•			•	•
Star Songs	83			•		•			•	•
Hot Spot	84	•				•			•	•
Static Relay	85	•			•				•	•
Seven Up	87			•	•			•		
Four Square	88		•		•				•	•
The Mannequin	89	•			•				•	
X-ray Vision	91			•	•			•		•
Little Professors, Little Einsteins	92			•		•			•	•
A Few of My Favorite Things	94			•	•			•		•
Etiquette Relay	95			•		•			•	•
Cultural Investigators	96	•			•			•		•
Colorful Scavenger Hunt	98			•	•				•	•
Bring on the Band	100	•			•				•	•
Magazine Drama	101			•		•			•	•
Rhyming Words	102			•	•			•		•
Name That Song	104			•	•			•		•
Name That Show	105			•	•				•	•
Celebrity Dress-up	106	•			•				•	•
Draw-off	107			•	•			•		•
Film Writers	109			•	•			•		•
Playdough Film Studio	110	•				•		•		•
Box Art	111	•			•			•		•

GAME TITLE	PAGE	LOCATION			RISK LEVEL			ENERGY LEVEL		SUPPLIES
		INSIDE	OUTSIDE	IN/OUT	LOW	MED	HIGH	SITTING	MOVING	
Topical Poets	112	•			•			•		•
Song Rewrites	113			•		•		•		•
Thumbprint Art Circles	114	•			•			•		•
Superhero Teams Relay Run	116			•	•				•	•
Animal Relay	117			•	•				•	•
Toss and Roll	119			•	•				•	•
Kick the Can	120		•		•				•	•
Paper-Wad Fun	121			•	•				•	•
Spinning Tops	122			•	•				•	•
Wacky Eating Relays	123			•	•				•	•
Balloon Sculptures	125	•			•			•		•
Balloon Gather	126	•			•				•	•
Soccer Balloon Dribble Race	127	•			•				•	•
Doggie Balloon Frolic	128	•			•				•	•
Balloon Wheelbarrow	129	•			•				•	•
Mr. Spider	131			•	•				•	
Tennis Baseball	132		•		•				•	•
Crazy Ball	133		•		•				•	•
Water Balloon Batting Practice	134		•		•				•	•
Follow the Leader Goes to the Playground	135			•	•				•	•
Snow Fight	137			•	•				•	•
Marshmallow Monsters	138			•	•			•		•
Marshmallow Sculptures	139			•	•			•		•
Marshmallow Olympics	140			•	•				•	•
Cup Pass	143		•		•				•	•
Water Relay	145		•		•				•	•
My Face Page	150	•				•			•	•
Whose Story Is It?	152			•		•		•		•
My Experiences	152			•		•		•		•
Famous for Values	154	•				•		•		•
PBJ Matches	155			•	•				•	•
Crisscross Circle	157			•		•			•	•
Spinners	158			•		•		•		•
Goldilocks and the Three Bears	159			•		•			•	•
Nursery Rhymes Quiz	161			•		•		•		•
Ooey Shoey Sharing	162	•			•				•	•
Beehive	163			•	•				•	•

GAME TITLE	PAGE	LOCATION			RISK LEVEL			ENERGY LEVEL		SUPPLIES
		INSIDE	OUTSIDE	IN/OUT	LOW	MED	HIGH	SITTING	MOVING	
Dumpty Humpty	164			•	•			•		•
The Animal Game	166			•		•			•	
Prince Charming Race	169			•	•				•	•
Matched Sets	170			•	•			•		•
Run, Rabbit, Run	172			•	•				•	•
Trio Battles	173			•	•				•	
Radio Songs	174			•		•		•		
Balloon Stomp	175			•	•				•	•
The Entertainment Committee	176			•		•			•	
Superhero Obstacle Course	177			•	•				•	
Snap, Crackle, Pop	178			•		•			•	
Double Concentration	179			•		•		•		•
Bottle Bowling	180	•			•				•	•
Alphabet Scavenger Hunt	182			•	•				•	
Coin Spellers	183			•	•				•	•
Build a Tower	184			•	•				•	•
High Speed	186			•	•				•	•
Mini-Tech Hunt	187	•			•			•		•
Tiddly Buttons	189			•	•			•		•
Blind Balance	190			•		•			•	•
Beach Ball Volley	191			•		•			•	•
Racetrack	192			•	•				•	•
Flight School	194			•		•			•	•
Walk Across the Country	196			•		•			•	•
All Toss	198			•		•			•	•
Thumbkins Appreciation	201			•		•		•		•
Freeze Frame	203			•		•			•	•
Canvas Word Art	204			•		•		•		•
Kaleidoscope	205	•				•			•	•
Balloon Skipping	207	•			•				•	•
Royal Affirmations	208			•		•			•	•
Celebration Meter	210			•		•		•		
Opposite Ends	211			•		•			•	
Rainmakers	212	•			•				•	
Shuffle, Shuffle	214			•		•			•	
H$_2$O	216			•	•			•		
Snack Attack	217			•	•			•		•
Alien Dancers	218			•	•				•	•

About the Authors

SUSAN RAGSDALE co-founded and directs the Center for Asset Development at the YMCA. Susan has directed middle Tennessee and national youth development initiatives at the YMCA since 1992. Two of her all-time favorite career highlights were her years helping coach the Bulldawgs, an inner-city sports team, and her time as a regional director for a youth environmental service-learning program.

Susan's fondness for using games to actively engage others begins with memories of her third- and fourth-grade teachers, Ms. Colleen and Mrs. Martin, respectively, who made learning fun by playing Spelling Baseball and History Jeopardy. As a 14-year-old summer sports camp counselor, she created wacky games to keep the campers—only two years younger!—moving and having a good time. Susan discovered that games were a fun way to explore life lessons, and she's been using games to build groups ever since. Susan lives in Nashville, Tennessee, with her husband, Pete, and their two dogs.

ANN SAYLOR has been teaching and writing in the youth and community development field since 1993. Before co-founding the Center for Asset Development, Ann enjoyed directing service-learning programs and empowering youth with the Points of Light Institute, Volunteer Tennessee, 4-H, and Harpeth Hall School. Ann lives in Pleasant View, Tennessee, with her husband, Dan, and their three children.

Ann's fascination with games began when she looked for new ways to teach teens and adults in classrooms, camps, and conferences. Realizing that most people (herself included) learn more effectively when they're active, experimenting with new behaviors, and solving challenges, she started collecting educational games from colleagues and friends. She never dreamed her folders filled with games would turn into a book!

Susan and Ann have worked together since 1999, when they co-hosted a national environmental conference. Since 2002, they have been leading workshops, developing curriculum, coaching organizations, and following their passion to author books. They invite you to visit their Web site and blog at www.TheAssetEdge.net and send your favorite games, tips, and ideas to them at cad@TheAssetEdge.net. You can also Twitter with them @TheAssetEdge.